Heroic Leadership

Jim Davis

First published in 2022 by Jim Davis

© Jim Davis
The moral rights of the author have been asserted.
This book is an Inspirational Book Writers book.

Author:
Davis, Jim

Title:
Heroic Leadership

ISBN:
978-1-4717-7901-5

All rights reserved. Except as permitted under the Australian Copyright Act 1968 (for example, a fair dealing for the purposes of study, research, criticism or review), no part of this book may be reproduced, stored in a retrieval system, communicated or transmitted in any form or by any means without prior written permission. All enquiries should be made to the author at *jim@jimdavislive.com*

Editor-in-chief: Anita Saunders
Cover Design: Sarah Rose Graphic Design

Disclaimer:
The material in this publication is of the nature of general professional advice, but it is not intended to provide specific guidance for particular circumstances and it should not be relied on as the basis for any decision to take action or not take action on any particular matter which it covers. Readers should obtain individual advice from the author where appropriate, before making any such decision. To the maximum extent permitted by law, the author and publisher disclaim all responsibility and liability to any person, arising directly or indirectly from any person taking or not taking action based on the information in this publication.

Dedicated to my wife and daughter, who continue to inspire me to be better and, maybe, just maybe, even heroic.

To my dad, who has always been, and will always be, my personal hero.

To all those daring souls listed in the pages of history, who, while ordinary, lived extraordinary lives and changed the world with their vision, courage, and tenacity.

Their heroic lives speak to us still today.

And to my readers. Thank you.

Remember, there's a hero in all of us.

Table of Contents

FOREWORD vii

AUTHOR'S NOTE ix

CHAPTER 1 – THE POWER OF VISION 1

CHAPTER 2 – THE STRENGTH TO WIN 17

CHAPTER 3 – THE VALUE OF TRUST 35

CHAPTER 4 – THE PRICE OF PROWESS 53

CHAPTER 5 – THE PASSION OF A JUST CAUSE 77

CHAPTER 6 – THE REALITY OF HOPE 93

CHAPTER 7 – THE HONOR OF FIGHTING FAIR 109

CHAPTER 8 – THE LEVELING OF CALM 127

CHAPTER 9 – A HEART TO SERVE 143

EPILOGUE 161

Foreword

The word hero gets tossed around far too casually.

Someone stops to help someone change a tire by the side of the road. Someone catches it on video, and they are called a hero.

A Hollywood celebrity takes five minutes to talk with someone with a terminal disease and they are called a hero.

A dog barks when there's a fire in the house and the dog is also labeled a hero.

Doing the right thing at the right time doesn't make anybody a hero.

Doing the extraordinary, when the situation is difficult, is what makes people truly heroic.

This is why we need this book.

Everyone has the capacity to be heroic. What people need right now is a guide on how to be extraordinary, when those surrounding them are content with being mediocre.

This is that guide.

If you want to live an extraordinary life, read this book.

If you are really busy and need reminders, start with the epilogue, which is a great list of what to do TODAY to be extraordinary.

All too often we witness what seems to be a sense of complacency and a general lack of effort. Jim shows us that does not have to be the norm.

As someone who spent 25 years on active duty in the United States Navy, I witnessed true acts of heroism- people who sacrificed for others, people who saved others, people who made decisions that were unpopular.

But they were the right decisions.

Being a hero means standing up for what is right and being a beacon for others to emulate.

Jim shows us how very ordinary people can accomplish extraordinary things when they decide to implement the practices in this book and live a heroic life.

Commander Mary C. Kelly,
US Navy (ret), Hall of Fame Speaker

Author's Note

We can be heroes
—David Bowie.

Heroes.

What thought enters your mind when you read that word? What image appears?

I know the world is full of them: regular individuals who sacrifice, work hard, serve others, and leave a tremendous impression on the lives of others every single day.

Heroes don't need capes. They don't need super strength, or the ability to fly, disappear, (or make others disappear). They don't need utility belts or magic rings. They don't need to be able to leap buildings or stop a speeding bullet.

Heroes don't need to be super to impact others for good.

We are all merely mortal. But we can all be heroes.

Super is a relative term. From the idea's very conception these extraordinary, though fictional, so-called powers have been on vivid display in the never-ending fight for truth and justice. Writers created stories and characters that would inspire and give hope to generation after generation, especially in difficult times. Many, for example, would credit the dime store comic books, in part, for keeping them inspired and their spirits buoyed throughout the Great Depression.

Heroes lift the souls of those who read about their stories of bravery and the causes they champion at every turn of the page. Villainy must be vanquished, just as the challenges in everyday life we all face.

"Superheroes" represent the uncommon strength and daring necessary to overcome "evil" with good—to save and rescue the defenseless against would-be world beaters or impending disasters. They make for great stories and happy reading.

But that's *fiction*.

Having said that, art can imitate life and the same can be said in reverse. While you and I will never have to battle a giant monster or horde of invading aliens, every story has an antagonist. Challenges and conflict are a part of our journey (as you will read in a later chapter).

For those you lead, not only can you be the hero in *their* story, but you can help them find the same in and for themselves. Ordinary people can do *extraordinary* things if they are inspired and led to do so.

That's the power and promise of heroic leadership.

What can be said about leadership that hasn't been already?

Thousands and thousands of books have been written on the subject, and many more valuable lessons can be learned from those who were terribly good leaders and those who were just plain terrible.

For anyone who aspires to be in the former category, the journey continues. While principles stay the same, the times

Author's Note

do not. But time *does* march on. And some lessons can easily fade and be forgotten like yellowed pages of a comic book.

But that's another reason leadership is so important and so vital. In every season, in every era, there is a monumental need for someone to rise to the occasion and provide positive, directive action as to be a part of the story of promise for that generation. While there have been leaders we admire, and leaders we'd sooner forget, all can serve as examples of the amazing capacity of influence.

The subject of leadership can be so mystical, and it shouldn't be. As this book will outline, it is not only for the chosen few. It is not a privileged gift bestowed on the select. It is something anyone can learn, practice, and perfect.

While superheroes are fictional, history is full of flawed men and women who influenced the masses in epic, future-altering ways. There are too many voices from the past that can illuminate both the present and the future to not be stirred and commit to be all that one can be in service to others. There are too many success stories, as well as those of mistakes and epic failures, to discount or devalue the tremendous import of leadership.

Heroes can come from every era and create stories that will be recalled long after they have departed the scene. Just as stories of colorful characters have filled the pages of a comic book, real people have lined the history books and have inspired readers for decades. You can do the same for those you serve.

This book will give you a sense of what made these individuals truly heroic. While there is no perfect leader, there is an ideal that every individual who seeks to persuade others can, and should, embrace.

My first foray into leadership was at a time in my life when I was young and foolish enough to think I knew much more than I did. Arrogance is *not* a winning trait for a leader.

But I was smart enough (thankfully) to begin reading and learning from mentors who were ahead of me. Much of what was learned was unlearned—a reprogramming of sorts that, providentially, occurred before too many bad habits set in.

This is part of why I wanted to write this book. I would have liked my 23-year-old self to have read what is in these pages. If you've ever doubted your potential, if you've wondered if you possess what it takes to be effective at influencing others, if you have dreams and aspirations for leading in a heroic, life-changing way, read on.

This book is for you.

You will discover what these ordinary heroes and world changers can teach us all.

Chapter 1

THE POWER OF VISION

Chapter 1
The Power of Vision

Where there is no vision, the people perish
—Proverbs.

It all starts with something better. Or, at least, it should. That's the power of vision.

Vision is simply a snapshot, or image, of a preferable future. It's the way things can be, ought to be, and *will* be, if impassionedly pursued.

The concept of heroes and their sense of idealism represents something more. Something better. It can help us see beyond the now into our best tomorrow.

Vision is the ability and awareness that prompted non-powered individuals to create, invent, and otherwise shape the future in truly remarkable ways.

The ripple effect from their vision still resounds today: the capacity to see and pursue the potential of a dream or an idea and transform what began as a thought into reality. That's the seemingly magical power of vision.

Davinci saw the idea of a machine gun, a parachute, even a mechanical knight long before any such devices were ever made.

Edison's idea of sound to be captured by a mechanical device and played back led to the invention of the phonograph. (You already know about the lightbulb.)

Henry Ford wanted every family to be able to own an automobile, because, at the time, only the wealthy could afford one. This led to the innovation of the assembly line and mass production.

Walt Disney, as a young man, frequented amusement parks and found them to be dirty, unfriendly, and not fun at all. He wanted to create a place where families could go, forget about their troubles for a day, and visit a place that was truly happy. His creation would eventually be known as "The Happiest Place on Earth."

Martin Luther King, Jr. saw a day in America when everyone, regardless of race, creed, or color could, and would, come together in a spirit of love and brotherhood and overcome base prejudice and bias.

Mother Teresa, moved by compassion, formed a group that would become The Missionaries of Charity, which serves the needy in 139 countries and has over 5,000 members.

Steve Jobs wanted to put a "ding in the universe" and, before that, a computer for the *rest of us*. There are currently over 100 million iPhone users.

The Wright Brothers believed man could fly when very few of their contemporaries were even interested in man-powered flight. They persevered through many, many setbacks to see that dream fulfilled.

There are certainly others, but all of these, and more, envisioned, created, invented, and developed modern wonders, all from a need or inspired idea that, in many cases, changed the world.

That's the power of vision. And it's not a superpower.

We choose to go to the Moon!

We choose to go to the Moon ... We choose to go to the Moon in this decade and do the other things, not because they are easy, but because they are hard; because that goal will serve to organize and measure the best of our energies and skills, because that challenge is one that we are willing to accept, one we are unwilling to postpone, and one we intend to win, and the others, too—John F. Kennedy.

This speech, given by President Kennedy, at a stadium at Rice University, was a rousing oration outlining the importance of looking ahead to what, at the time, seemed like a distant, impossible dream, putting a man on the moon.

Up to that point the United States was far behind in the space race. The Soviets had successfully launched the rocket "Sputnik" four years earlier, making Yuri Gagarin the first man in space and, by default, the Russians.

President Kennedy not only wanted to match what the Soviets had achieved, he believed the US could surpass it. He told Congress he wanted to send a man to the moon and return him safely before the decade was out.

In other words, he was saying, "Why not us?"

That's the motivational value of any clear and compelling vision. It provides a clear compass and a focused aim that would rather fire and miss than not at all. For Kennedy, as a leader, it was a masterful use of the presidential pulpit to tap into the legacy of the American pioneering spirit and leverage its history with the potential to create the future and write a new and exciting chapter.

Kennedy understood and believed his words could persuade the populace to support the United States' space program in its efforts to put a man on the moon.

Vision can, and should be, more than just a nice idea or fuzzy concept. It shouldn't be so easy to discount the idea of becoming and achieving more. There's just too much possibility in powerfully painting and presenting what people can become to marginalize it.

Without it, life and work will slip into the mundane. Clearly not every business and leader will succeed, and often it can be traced to a lack of vision.

In his book, *The Power of Vision* (nice title), George Barna states:

A business without vision is like a flashlight without batteries; powerless and unable to light the way.

This leaves teams in the dark and uncertain about the future. Heroic leaders can "see" into an endless set of probabilities as future tomorrows unfold.

That's the power of vision.

> *Heroic leaders can "see" into an endless set of probabilities.*

Why is vision so important?

Vision directs. A clear vision is like a virtual travel guide. It indicates direction to a specific and targeted destination. It guards against what could be described as the *driftwood mentality* which causes one to basically float with each new wave, as there is no effort in coasting.

Leaders fight against the tide and sail on more purposefully.

There's a well-worn adage that states *if you don't know your destination, any road will get you there*. Visionaries take a more deliberate, strategic approach. Visionary leaders have the future in their sights first, then chart the course to follow.

As one last footnote: While the actuality of putting a man on the moon was not fully realized until Neil Armstrong, Michael Collins, and "Buzz" Aldrin Jr. landed in July 1969, the path was set. The challenge had been made. The route to the future was underway and ultimately realized.

Vision prompts necessary and inspired action, positive and optimistic activeness.

When **Jim Carrey** was unknown and unemployed, he wrote a check to himself to the amount of 10 million dollars. In the memo section he wrote "for acting services rendered." He's now worth 20 times that.

Phillip Rivers, the Indianapolis Colts quarterback, as a child, put a picture of himself on the body of a professional NFL player.

While some may see these acts as silly, or even contrived, it crystalizes the desired goal and objective for the mind to visualize and affirm. If you can't stop thinking about it, you shouldn't stop working for it.

Vision bolsters excellence. It gives people something big to do and brings out the best in who they are. It elevates their performance. Vision transcends normal capacity and stretches ability. Vision causes individuals and groups to be better than they ever thought they could be.

Recently one of what is considered the greatest sporting events in history (especially in the Olympics) celebrated its 40th anniversary: the "Miracle on Ice." On February 22, 1980, a group of mostly amateur US hockey players shockingly defeated a group of largely professional Soviet players during the Winter Olympics. The Soviets had dominated the sport, winning the last four winter games.

Was it luck? Some may try to attribute this unbelievable achievement to the law of probability, given the fact that the Russians had crushed that same American team in an earlier exhibition.

But the more likely scenario is, in part, tied to the visionary pre-game speech delivered by coach Herb Brooks which included the powerful statement *great moments are born from great opportunity*.

This was one of those great opportunities, and the players could picture, in their mind, and even down to their soul, an impossible win over a superior, virtually unbeatable, team.

That's the power of *visioneering*: seeing and communicating something you and your team could be and do and more than you previously imagined. It's an elevating dynamic.

No team gets excited about a coach that shrugs his shoulders and talks about remaining average or accepting and maintaining the status quo.

A strong vision will elevate and cause people to be more and do more.

> *Vision makes people better than they ever thought they could be.*

Vision refines motivation. Does that matter? Isn't motivation another one of those fluffy terms that can be found on some artsy picture on the wall? The short answer is no. Motivation is the reason that someone does, or doesn't, do a something. During times of grinding effort, the mundane can take over the sense of what was once inspiration and the *why* behind the *what* becomes as important as fuel is to an engine.

Motivation *is* intrinsic but can be greatly enhanced with a view of what's ahead if it's clear and captivating. No doubt, during the space race, there were many Americans who were frustrated, perhaps angry, that the Soviets were, in their minds, beating the US. This helped energize the effort to not only enter the race but *win* it. But it all started with the idea that it could actually be done. Not easily, but eventually. President Kennedy excelled at explaining the why, even in the face of a difficult path forward, and spurred a nation toward a lofty goal.

Vision clarifies. There should be no doubt regarding the importance of focus. Life and work are notoriously filled with distractions ranging in importance as well as perceived urgency.

Everything, including one's leadership, is stronger when focused. Consider water pressure, heat, light, a laser: all more powerful when narrowed. Who didn't take a magnifying glass outside in the summer sun to burn leaves? Hopefully no fires were started!

Similarly, a strong vision will deftly sharpen the aim and help master decision-making as to what to permit and what to deny. It's common knowledge that everything that is urgent is not always important and what is important is not always urgent. (Thank you, Dwight Eisenhower.)

Clarity and single-mindedness will strengthen every leader and the potential for success of any project or objective. No one likes to swim in murky waters.

Focus not only clarifies what to do, but also what not to do. Much time and energy can be saved by following a clearly-defined vision.

> *No one wants to swim in murky waters.*

Vision unites. It's a rallying point for any group committed to a common cause (more on that later.) A strong vision combats the toxic effect of personal or hidden agendas. To achieve real group success *every* team member should be wholly committed to the mission of the organization, and not just out of pure obligation.

A compelling vision, attached to the reason a group exists in the first place, will move members and followers from mere compliance to *commitment*. The more that are genuinely dedicated, rather than minimally agreeable from a sense of fear or duty, the stronger will be the unit and grander the achievement.

President Kennedy knew this. He used his moon speech as a rallying cry for Americans to work together to achieve the vision of space travel. Vision can effectively bridge the past, present, and future together in a way that truly brings, and keeps, people together.

Vision is more than just blue-sky thinking or a pretentious idea. The acid test is how this *preferable future* is credibly and enthusiastically pursued. How many such dreams die a painful death in an imaginary waiting room or, worse, the prison of inaction? Action separates those who did something from those who *almost* did.

However, it's worth noting that there are some leadership landmines along the way, all based on assumptions, which can easily be eliminated with quality and assertive communication.

Vision Trap #1: *Assuming everyone will love the vision*. Everyone will *not* love it. Cast it anyway. The reality is some may *hate* your vision. Some may fear it or, at the very least, question it. Most leaders tend to be idealistic and the pushback from those who don't share in your ideology can be like a cold splash of water to the face.

If vision involves growth, then it stands to reason that it involves change and a higher level of commitment. A forward vision challenges the comfort zone that so many individuals have built and where they pleasantly reside.

Growth and comfort are not mutual. Vision and the status quo are polar opposites. It's not enough to bemoan and besmirch those who don't immediately appreciate the new picture of their future until they are able to adjust their eyes and allow their heart and mind to catch up.

Realize not everyone will immediately embrace your vision. Cast it anyway and lead on.

A forward vision challenges the comfort zone that so many individuals have built and in which they pleasantly reside.

Vision Trap #2: *Assuming everyone will support the vision*. Is it possible to find value in a leader's proposed direction and still not support it? Of course. Levels of support can vary wildly. This is why one shouldn't attempt to lead by taking polls. Vision is given to a *person* not a committee. One doesn't vote on a vision; one creates, then imparts, the vision.

Vision is not the *result* of consensus but should result *in* consensus. Big difference. There will always be "armchair quarterbacks" who may criticize some of the finer points or boast about how their approach is better. That tension will remain a constant between leaders and followers.

Note to self: *Never* let anyone hijack your vision. Fight for it. Protect it.

That said, the great privilege and opportunity of every leader is to help those they serve overcome their doubts and perceived challenges and take the plunge into that preferable future. It's a risk well worth taking.

Vision is not the result of consensus but should result in consensus.

Vision Trap #3: Assuming that saying it once is enough. Vision *leaks*. People forget. They get busy. They *are* busy. Aside from that reality, how important will hearers consider a vision statement that is only conveyed once or twice without increased frequency?

If the vision is important, it must be constantly promoted. Always keep the vision front and center using every means available. Failure to do so can be one reason that disconnect can occur between the idea and the daily pursuit that should follow.

Silence creates gap.

Pursuit of a preferable future can dramatically change and elevate a culture and behavior, but not without keeping the vision in the forefront and top of mind. People want to be inspired, motivated, and excited about something or somewhere better than present reality.

Today is the sum of the active quest of yesterday's visionary leaders.

What is your vision for tomorrow's reality? What is that *preferable future* you're charting?

Is it big enough to excite your team and break them out of the ordinary and what's comfortable?

What new idea or creation is speaking to you and prompting you to start (or restart) something that could touch the world around you?

Focus on that image that could be a little fuzzy, at first, but can become very clear with a step or two in the right direction.

Don't be afraid to exercise the power of vision. Your better tomorrow awaits.

The Power of Vision

* Vision is a snapshot of a preferable future.
* Vision directs, clarifies, and empowers.
* Vision takes people out of their comfort zone.
* Not everyone will love your vision.
* Vision does not result from consensus but should result in consensus.
* Never let anyone hijack your vision. Fight for it. Protect it.
* Vision leaks. People forget. Never assume saying it once is enough.

Chapter 2

THE STRENGTH TO WIN

Chapter 2
The Strength to Win

Winning is fun ... Sure. But winning is not the point.
Wanting to win is the point.
Not giving up is the point. Never letting up is the point.
Never being satisfied with what you've done is the point
—Pat Summitt.

One thing is clear regarding any hero we admire, real or fictional: *We expect them to win.* It's basically assumed. Big bright costume, super ability, dramatic music, (just imagine that part), and it's anticipated that he or she will find a way to defy the odds and be victorious in the end. Cue the music again.

No matter the story, foe, or situation, each hero, we believe, will eventually prove to be the champion we all knew he or she could be. The certainty and anticipation of victory is tied to the strength every hero displays, even in the face of dire straits or great adversity. This is just one reason heroes are so celebrated and revered.

The same can be said of us ordinary folk. Remember, no cape required. The strength to win comes from the state of mind and attitude of the heart that says *I can*. This doesn't mean fluffy self-talk or spouting clichés or silly mantras.

The strength to win is an attitude and a spirit that will not allow a person to live under the circumstances but rise above them with a resilient refusal to lose.

Name almost any athlete that is renowned for their number of wins and championships and history will answer with a stack of statistics that will balance the scale regarding losses and failures.

Babe Ruth hit 714 career homeruns but also struck out 1330 times. But what do we remember about the *Sultan of Swat*?

Michael Jordan made a game-winning shot in the NBA 25 times and scored the winning basket in the 1982 NCAA Tournament. But he also missed 9,000 shots in his career, lost 300 games, and missed 26 of those times that it was all up to him in a game's closing seconds. But what do we remember about arguably the greatest NBA player of all time? Six world championships.

Even **Muhammad Ali** lost five times in his career, but what do remember about the one who called himself *the greatest*? That he *was* the greatest.

No one is exempt from losses. They can't be avoided, and every individual must brace and stand ready.

The human spirit can, and should, stand tall and bravely face every set of challenges and fight to prevail. We run the race to win, to finish.

Surrender should never be an option. We certainly wouldn't remember these sports legends well, or at all, had they thrown down the bat or taken their ball and gone home after a few failed attempts.

In the same way, people are looking for leaders who possess the clear resolve to triumph, not concede defeat. Everyone wants to follow a winner, to rely on a leader who knows how to win and will inspire the kind of confidence every person needs to face what each day will bring.

Everyone can be that heroic leader *if* they possess the strength to win.

Winston Churchill was that kind of leader. And given he's one of my favorite people of all time, he gets a lot of ink in this book. Buckle up for some history!

Winston Churchill is largely regarded as one of the most consequential leaders of the 20th century. His role and impact during World War II remains one of the greatest testaments to the power of transformative leadership not only at the time, but for future generations.

Churchill's talent and ability as a reassuring orator, his love of country, and his no-nonsense approach to politics certainly were contributing factors to his powerful leadership and legacy.

But at the root of it all, Winston Churchill was committed to winning. He radiated the importance of a positive, indomitable spirit, even in the face of mortal danger.

When the world was at war and his country was being decimated by artillery, Winston Churchill exuded the kind of strength and poise that was a stark contrast to the overwhelming circumstances, which is just one example of effective leadership. His attitude and his words rallied a nation as bombs leveled cities.

This strength was nothing new to the gritty prime minister. During World War I he was known to set up his easel and paint near the front lines as shells exploded just feet away.

Could there be any better picture of choosing a contrarian attitude than that?

> *Everyone wants to follow a winner.*

Winning is an attitude before it's reality.

While the subject of a winning attitude has been covered extensively, its value cannot be understated or underestimated. Researchers have concluded that one's attitude represents 85% of overall success. It wouldn't even be a stretch to say that attitude is *everything*.

It carries that much impact.

Churchill bravely decided not to allow the horrors of war to limit his mindset or detract from his optimistic message to the nation and the world. But this perspective wasn't developed during these moments of global conflict. It was simply *demonstrated* during the most trying of times, and on the biggest stage possible.

Winston Churchill did not become the fierce leader and conqueror by skating through life.

While it would be easy to say his was a comfortable one, given that he was born into relative wealth and social status, Churchill's early years were nothing if not challenging.

As a schoolchild Churchill had to deal with a speech impediment as well as what many historians have concluded to be dyslexia. Although considered intelligent, he was often lonely and performed at the bottom of his class.

Churchill struggled saying words that began with the letter "s." He often found himself alone and detached from his classmates. Even his mother was scarce in visiting during his schooling.

Add to that Churchill's impulsive energy, his early education was another lesson in contrast. How did someone who was destined to become one of the greatest strategic minds in world history receive such low marks in class? The good that came out of this was that Churchill put his energy into subjects that he enjoyed—a remedy that would help prepare him for later life.

Churchill would learn to be a winner even in the harsh aftermath of bitter failure. Near the end of World War I, as Secretary of the Royal Navy, Churchill proposed a military strategy designed to take control of the waterways in the area that is now Turkey. This would link the Black Sea and the Mediterranean and give the British unimpeded access to one of their allies, Russia.

The War Cabinet supported the plan even though all knew the price would be heavy. It was estimated that an army of 50,000 and strong naval strength would be needed to achieve the objective.

Unfortunately, the result dramatically failed to meet expectation. Due to several missteps, not the least of which was the War Office sending an insufficient number of troops, history remembers the Gallipoli Campaign as an unqualified disaster. Ultimately this doomed operation dragged on for nine months with the Allies losing over 45,000 troops.

The effect of this defeat was felt immediately. It brought turmoil to the government and Churchill became the scapegoat. This had to be a difficult pill for the burgeoning political leader to swallow as he considered himself a rising military strategist.

While removed from his government position and reassigned to an obscure post, Churchill was able to process through the shock of his failure and feelings of resignation and, once again, find a solution that would reassign his personal priorities and allow him to rise above a frustrated season in life.

The decision and action Churchill decided to take may have surprised some, but, perhaps, not those who knew him best. Churchill decided to join the infantry and go to the front lines.

He could have retired to the quiet life the government and station assigned him and live out his life to process his feeling of disappointment and disgrace. That is extremely unfulfilling, however, and Winston Churchill possessed too much personal fortitude and pluck to accept that sad a fate.

Churchill realized what every winner must: failure is not final, nor does it have to prove *fatal*.

The Gallipoli Campaign fiasco was a devastating loss in every way. It certainly seemed like a career ender just on its face. For many it would have been, the humiliation proving overwhelming.

> *Failure is not final,
> nor does it have to prove fatal.*

While Churchill was out of government, during the 1930s, he remained connected to the British people in a way that would serve him well as their future leader.

History tells us that Neville Chamberlain, the prime minister serving at the time of the Nazi regime, failed to fully appreciate and accurately assess the warning signs and the potential threat coming from Germany. In May of 1940 he scheduled a meeting with two individuals: Lord Halifax and none other than Winston Churchill. Chamberlain planned to resign and wanted to speak with the two men, one of which would likely succeed him.

When offered the position, Halifax declined. Churchill was more than happy to accept. On May 10 Winston Churchill was appointed as England's 70th prime minister. He became England's leader at a time when his countrymen needed him the most. The world was plunged into another war and the people of Great Britain needed a fighter, someone who knew how to rise to a challenge.

They needed a victor.

They would find one in Winston Churchill who would later become known as "the British Bulldog," in part, because of his great tenacity and refusal to surrender, even in the face of utter destruction and devastation.

Churchill was tested early and often. For example, from September 1940 to May 1941 London was bombed by the Germans mercilessly. This offensive was known as Blitzkrieg, or "lightning war," a name shortened to "Blitz." The purpose of the campaign was to gain air superiority.

While, ultimately, this was considered by most somewhat of a strategic failure for the Germans, it did result in the loss of 40,000 lives and more than a million homes destroyed or damaged.

Churchill's leadership proved to be more than strategy and organization. He knew how to rouse confidence even in the face of danger and utter destruction.

In one of his most notable speeches, given June 4, 1940, he said the following:

I have, myself, full confidence that if all do their duty, if nothing is neglected, and if the best arrangements are made, as they are being made, we shall prove ourselves once again able to defend our Island home, to ride out the storm of war, and to outlive the menace of tyranny, if necessary for years, if necessary alone.

At any rate, that is what we are going to try to do. That is the resolve of His Majesty's Government—every man of them. That is the will of Parliament and the nation.

The British Empire and the French Republic, linked together in their cause and in their need, will defend to the death their native soil, aiding each other like good comrades to the utmost of their strength.

Even though large tracts of Europe and many old and famous States have fallen or may fall into the grip of the Gestapo and all the odious apparatus of Nazi rule, we shall not flag or fail.

The Strength to Win

We shall go on to the end, we shall fight in France,
we shall fight on the seas and oceans,
we shall fight with growing confidence and growing strength in the air, we
shall defend our Island, whatever the cost may be,
we shall fight on the beaches,
we shall fight on the landing grounds,
we shall fight in the fields and in the streets,
we shall fight in the hills;
we shall never surrender, and even if, which I do not for a moment
believe, this Island or a large part of it were subjugated and starving,
then our Empire beyond the seas, armed and guarded by the British
Fleet, would carry on the struggle, until, in God's good time, the New
World, with all its power and might, steps forth to the rescue and the
liberation of the old.

Churchill was a stark contrast to his predecessor.

While Chamberlain will be remembered as a passive, timid leader, it didn't take long for the United Kingdom to learn what it meant to be led by a prevailing one. Even now your mind might be recalling pictures of Churchill holding up his two fingers showing "V" for victory.

Churchill exuded confidence and dogged determination. While he infuriated some, he inspired many more. He was exactly the type of tough-minded leader England needed now in her history, and that of the world.

Victory is seen in the mind before it is visible to others. In Churchill's thought processes, there was never any doubt that England, and her allies, could win, and should win. He stated: *Victory at all costs, victory in spite of all terror, victory however long and hard the road may be; for without victory, there is no survival.*

Every effective leader must have the same commitment to winning. While he was certainly making this statement in the shadow of a global war, the principle is the same. Victory must be won internally before it is evident elsewhere.

Far too many leaders allow external forces too much sway over their general disposition and outlook. The sequence is backwards. External forces should be influenced by an internal dynamic, not the other way around. Churchill demonstrated a tenacious spirit that allowed him to overcome his personal deficiencies and professional challenges.

How can his example serve the times in which we live? After all, principles are timeless and transferable. What did England's 70th prime minister exhibit that could make for stronger leadership in the 21st century?

Victory must be won internally before it's evident elsewhere.

Strength begins with a winning attitude.

Every individual possesses a potential for either defeat or victory. We honor our heroes because they enter the fray of battle drawing from their will to win at all costs. That sense of boldness and daring will not be easily overwhelmed by circumstance, even extremely adverse ones.

Attitude is a state of mind one chooses regardless of circumstance, not *because* of them.

And it is a *choice*. Attitude is not forced on you like a beast of burden. It's more like something you put on as you would a piece of clothing. It's an outward presentation of your inner self.

No one, or nothing, can make you feel a certain way.

Viktor Frankl, the Jewish psychiatrist and Holocaust survivor said this:

The one thing you can't take away from me is the way I choose to respond to what you do to me. The last of one's freedoms is to choose one's attitude in any given circumstance.

And he was a prisoner of war. One who had family members die in other camps and he, himself, separated from everyone he loved and everything he knew.

Frankl, just as Churchill, recognized that the greatest freedom and power one had in life is to choose one's attitude. Both these men had plenty of reasons and occasions to mull around in the dumpster of negative emotion, but they opted for a brighter disposition.

Everyone has that same freedom and power.

> *Attitude is a state of mind one chooses regardless of circumstance, not because of them.*

Focus on winning, not whining.

Whiners need pep talks, winners give pep talks. Whiners can talk themselves into the mire of complaining as they glare at what's wrong instead of possible solutions. Complaining, then, just becomes an end in itself.

As Randy Pausch states:

If you took one-tenth the energy you put into complaining and applied it to solving the problem you'd be surprised by how well things can work out. Complaining does not work as a strategy. We all have finite time and energy. Any time we spend whining is unlikely to help us achieve our goals. And it won't make us happier.

I've never met a happy complainer.

The eagle and the buzzard both find what they're looking for. Stay positive, think rationally, and don't let your mind race to all the worst-case scenarios without informing your perspective with healthy, not world-ending, thoughts. You will never be a positive person thinking that way.

Don't give up.

If there's one mantra that defined a big part of Churchill's legacy is his refusal to quit. The strength to win includes the repeated acts and demonstration of perseverance. While that can be an overused term and reduced to a hollow platitude, one can't argue against the need to persist in spite of strong headwinds.

For too many, it's just too easy to quit, check out, throw in the towel. And often it could be right at that moment when victory is at hand.

How many victories have been prematurely forfeited because the need to stop became greater than the desire to continue? The motivation simply gave out and a sense of resignation and submission took over.

Leadership can be a lonely and often arduous journey. The calling of every great individual can become overshadowed by feelings of fear, fatigue, and frustration.

Fear of failure, of not meeting others' expectations, of not reaching the finish line can be a very jolting and paralyzing emotion that will eventually stop you in your tracks.

Fatigue and burnout can happen virtually undetected until your head hits the wall and there's a sense of confusion about why you're not continuing to advance. Once that happens it's hard to relight the fuse.

Detracting emotions can dig deep into the psyche of every earnest leader and feel like a wet blanket or heavy weight as he or she faithfully plods along. Until he or she doesn't.

Learn to refuse to lose. Don't stop when victory is almost at hand. When you lose sight of the shore you will stop swimming. Winners enjoy the celebration in the circle while quitters are relegated to wonder what could have been.

Rest, but don't quit. People want to follow winners! Be that heroic leader.

One day you'll thank yourself for not giving up. And so will your team.

> *When you lose sight of the shore, you'll quit swimming.*

Talk about winning. A lot!

Imagine any sports team in any locker room right before the big game. Nerves are frayed, tension is thick, and anticipation has emotions running high. Also imagine the coach slumbering in with a long, somber look and saying something to the effect of, "Listen, I don't want to be here any more than you do, but we're here. Let's just go out and mark time, get through it, and go home at the end of it."

Who in that group would be enthused, fired up, or even slightly interested in taking the field or the court, prepared to sweat and even risk injury to win? Would you?

In Chapter 1 I wrote about how vision motivates and elevates people to be better than they ever thought they could be. The example I used was the 1980 US hockey team and the pre-game speech **Herb Brooks** gave.

His words certainly apply here.

Great moments are born from great opportunity.
And that's what you have here tonight, boys.
That's what you've earned here, tonight.
One game.
If we played 'em 10 times, they might win nine.
But not this game. Not tonight.
Tonight, we skate with 'em.
Tonight, we stay with 'em, and we shut them down because we can!
Tonight, we are the greatest hockey team in the world.
You were born to be hockey players—every one of ya.
And you were meant to be here tonight.
This is your time.
Their time—is done. It's over.
I'm sick and tired of hearin' about what a great hockey team the Soviets have. Screw 'em!
This is your time!!

Chances are you may be ready to take the ice!

For teams to truly win they have to hear it, feel it, and even taste it coming from their leader's mouth.

Both Brooks and Churchill had a way of talking about winning and victory in the face of overwhelming odds, when it would have been easier to simply accept the dim prospect of defeat.

Heroic leaders are not unrealistic. They don't practice blind optimism or wishful thinking. Instead, they choose to do all they can, drawing on the strength to win, to provide the best opportunity for victory and create a new world for themselves and those they serve.

Everyone wants to follow a winner.

Be that.

- Heroes are expected to win.
- Failure doesn't have to be fatal.
- Everyone wants to follow a winner.
- Attitude is chosen regardless of circumstance, not because of it.
- Be a winner not a whiner.
- Rest, but don't quit.
- Be vocal about winning. Sound the call.
- Winning often defies logic and circumstance.

Chapter 3

THE VALUE OF TRUST

Chapter 3
The Value of Trust

Trust each other again and again. When the trust level gets high enough, people transcend apparent limits, discovering new and awesome abilities of which they were previously unaware
—David Armistead.

Heroes can be counted on to show up. It might be just in the nick of time, or seconds before the locomotive reaches the damsel in distress, but part of why we celebrate them is that we believe they will, indeed, save the day.

That's trust. That's earned confidence. It's not given, it's *earned*. Honor can be bestowed based on position or status, but trust is different. Through valiant acts, both great and small, the individual in on the frontlines, leading the charge, can become the person who faithfully deserves that level of trust.

Trust is not automatic, and it is not magic. We trust another because we learn, over time, that he or she is worthy of it. We know they will do the right thing, *every* time. We trust those who come through, over and over, and we freely relate with, absent of any doubt, those who work hard to protect and cherish that confidence. We confide in another because we've given ourselves permission to do so. Otherwise, we simply look elsewhere, or, if given no choice, offer as much trust as the situation deserves and hope for the best.

For the heroic leader, trust is the foundation on which everything else is built. When trust is secure, communication is healthy, productivity is higher, as is morale, and the opportunities for group success are more readily available.

Work and life will provide either a strong underpinning for that kind of mutual success or become a breeding ground for suspicion. The latter gives way to weary and isolated lone rangers who fail to build the confidence in relationships that's paramount for group success.

As **Pete Drucker** states:

The leaders who work most effectively, it seems to me, never say 'I.' And that's not because they have trained themselves not to say 'I.' They don't think 'I.' They think 'we'; they think 'team.' They understand their job to be to make the team function. They accept responsibility and don't sidestep it, but 'we' gets the credit ... This is what creates trust, what enables you to get the task done.

While synergy is a somewhat dog-eared term, it doesn't have to fade because it may seem dated. Nor does it need to reside in mere idealism. However you choose to say it, obviously, more can be done by a group that fully relies on one another and values interdependence.

One is always too small a number for success.

Trust is not given. It's earned.

Climbing great heights together.

Tenzing Norgay knew the value of confidence in others long before he and Edmund Hillary finally reached the summit of Mt. Everest on May 29, 1953.

Norgay had been on six of these expeditions before joining this one. All of them failed.

Yet, these two men did, in fact, become the first two individuals to reach the top of this fabled mountain. But make no mistake; they certainly did not do it alone.

There were hundreds of people involved in this venture and every role was important, not the least of which was the management of thousands of pounds of baggage. Between 200 and 300 people were required just to get the supplies to camp. As the group ascended the more experienced Sherpas would continue to carry the equipment to higher locations.

The greater the elevation, the greater the skill and expertise that was needed, as well as the level of trust. If you did not work together on this kind of endeavor, someone could die.

Often people did.

Tenzing Norgay learned a great many things in all his attempts to climb Mt. Everest. The one lasting one was this:

No one climbs the mountain alone.

Teamwork can be such a commonplace expression and even sound like a cliché or buzzword.

If that's true, it might be because not enough people actually *experience* it. Maybe not everyone wants to allow themselves to trust another and be a devoted part of a team. But the imperative of unity cannot be overstated.

> *No one climbs the mountain alone.*

While we may not be planning to climb a nearly 30,000 ft. mountain anytime soon, confidence in our relationships with others is, nonetheless, just as important.

It is a value that must be caught, not taught. For that value to resonate, it must be demonstrated and practiced in all the highs and lows of daily life, or even during a national conflict.

"Of the People, By the People, For the People."

Even though he prefaced his comments with the sentiment that *few will remember what is said here*, the Gettysburg Address is widely known as one of Abraham Lincoln's most enduring speeches. Delivered November 19, 1863, the 16th president was there to dedicate the National Cemetery of Gettysburg in Pennsylvania.

He was not the main speaker. That honor fell to Edward Everett, renowned as one of the great orators of his day. Everett spoke for two hours, proving that it's not the *quantity* of words, but the *quality* which makes a speech remarkable. No one remembers what this supposed famed speaker said.

But in a speech that was two minutes, not two hours, every word Lincoln uttered was poignant and woven into the fabric of America's history. His remarks served as an impassioned plea for the unity by which the young nation originally fought to establish.

While all of the 272 words are profound, the last phrase, *and that government of the people, by the people, for the people, shall not perish from the earth* says much about the heart of a leader distraught by the fact that the country was so violently at war with itself.

In fact, the speech was delivered just four and a half months removed from the deadliest battles of the Civil War in which there were over 23,000 casualties.

This makes these closing words even more meaningful and relevant for the hour. Lincoln, who was heartbroken over the war, reminded the hearers of the reason America was founded in the first place. When he spoke of "the people" he was referencing *all* people, not the North or the South. Not just white or black, rich or poor, slave or free.

While Lincoln wanted the war to be over, and the bloodshed stopped, he wanted even more for the nation to be united once again. He loathed the fact that the blight of slavery became a dividing point for the country and spoke against it prior to his presidency saying,

A house divided against itself cannot stand.

He went on to express his belief that the nation could not continue being half slave and half free.

Indeed, he was correct.

Lincoln understood the dangers and mortal realities of national division and wanted to use his speech as a rallying cry to articulate why unity among his countrymen mattered so deeply.

This, at a time when brother fought against brother and mothers were losing their sons.

Lincoln was effective with context. He was a master at communicating. He found a way to honor the dead but also point to a time that America would, once again, unite in a way that would honor all the sacrifices made for freedom's sake.

People need a reason to place their trust and to attach themselves to another, or a group, who asks for their time, energy, and investment. There must be a central focus that draws individuals from different backgrounds, demographics, temperaments, and personalities to be and work together as one.

> *People need a reason to place their trust and to attach themselves to another.*

Lincoln espoused national sentiment hoping his message could be as ointment to an open wound. While it took something different to finally resolve the bloody conflict, Abraham Lincoln continued to harken to the verity of a united America, calling on his *undoubted friends* to work together to see that dream fulfilled once again.

A team divided is a team diminished. How can it *not* be? Unity is a force multiplier. When personal agendas or individualism creep in, collaboration is reduced, as is productivity. Morale also takes a beating.

The Value of Trust

While quotes and slogans come and go, "Teamwork makes the dream work" is one that can likely be found on quite a few walls in corporate offices (at least in days past, as that quote is around 30 years old or more).

It *is* true: teamwork *does* make the dream work. And it should. But obviously that isn't always the case. Because just as it is with trust, teamwork is not automatic. Teamwork is not something that transpires by osmosis or simply over time, void of effort.

Remember, trust has to be earned. It is not just a noun, but also a verb. The heroic leader must foster the right environment for concrete trust to be established and grow.

A team divided is a team diminished.

Building unity around what's most important to the mission *will* bring people together and *keep* them together. Yes, teamwork *can* make the dream work. But leaders don't rely solely on slogans. There must be something more profound than a rhyming phrase. Further, just preaching and simply expecting team unity is not enough. The Gettysburg Address was more than a speech. It represented years of advocating for, and dying for, the freedom and soul of a nation.

The character and heart of team members will always be a big factor in how the team, overall, even desires to perform *together*.

Of course, talking about working together in the spirit of trust is helpful. But more than that, the heroic leader will also work to develop the characteristics and actions necessary for a group of individuals to genuinely meld together. They will combat the sentiment of "easier said than done," a phrase all too often uttered within the halls of many organizations.

Any leader can put a group of people together, give them a task, assign a deadline, and leave the room. Has he or she created a team? No. Nothing of the sort has been created. No time for building trust has even expired. And make no mistake, it does take time.

Simply giving a group of individuals a project or task is simply that. They are all still individuals. Trust and unity take time and a commitment to something larger.

Abraham Lincoln valiantly strived to hold a nation at war together. Are there any greater issues, or points of division, in any board room, than those related to a violent national conflict?

How many visions and grand schemes have been sidelined and derailed because a group of individuals refused to move beyond their personal agendas and opinions and support the leader striving to be worthy of their trust?

So, what is a leader to do? Are words not important? How many speeches and talks about *working together* are given in staff meetings or all-hands meetings?

At the heart of trust is a desire, from all involved, to actually *be* a unit. We are, after all, human *beings*, not human *doings*. The act of growing that kind of confidence must take root internally before revealed externally.

The Value of Trust

There are plenty of employees and colleagues who feign team spirit but participate in passive-aggressive behavior once the spotlight is off. This can become a cancer that spreads and infects the best of groups. No doubt you've heard of the law of the bad apple.

Instruction is not enough. It can translate to *talk is cheap*. Words matter but are limited without both the nurturing of cooperation and a willingness of each team member.

Where does that will originate? There are certain traits and characteristics that need to reside within individuals for them to truly be a unit. There is a spirit of teamwork that comes from substance of character, not just trying harder.

This is where heroic leadership can raise the bar and the team. Any leader can grow and be a champion of trust and unity. He or she can model the kinds of shared values that will help any group be more than a team in name only.

It can't be faked. It can't be pretense. Trust doesn't work if it's fabricated or placated.

Trust and honesty go hand in hand. It's key to authentic leadership and must be rooted in character and integrity.

> *We are, after all, human beings, not human doings.*

The journey to building trust starts with self. It can begin by answering the following questions and answering with candid introspection.

How much can I be trusted? Assessment and feedback are vital in every area of personal growth, including personal trustworthiness. If you don't know, simply ask. Find a way to gather specific information on how much, and in key areas of trust you rate.

Why would anyone follow a person he or she deems not worthy of their trust?

The answer is they wouldn't. But maybe they do, maybe they don't. If they don't believe they can trust you, they can't, or won't follow. Or, at least, they won't *want* to.

When people follow you because they must, it can be a demoralizing and deflating experience. Productivity suffers and little to no empowerment or increase takes place. Nothing grows.

People need to feel secure with their choice to believe in you. Heroes *earn* that right; they don't *assume* it.

Heroic leaders understand that nothing can be taken for granted. There are too many dangers and holes found in the world of assumptions. Heroic leaders operate from a place of intent and understanding that they own the potential for a healthy and growing level of trust. They work hard to achieve it. They prove their competence, act with integrity, tell the truth, and are devoted and caring.

These are the marks of a leader who wants to genuinely build people, not just command and control. Your commitment to become that effective leader begins with understanding how your team perceives and is willing to trust you.

Ask. Don't leave it to chance.

The Value of Trust

How consistently do I do the right thing, not the easy thing? Integrity is paramount in leadership and building trust. It's the moral fiber of both. The business world doesn't need more leaders who are smart, talented, technical, or know how to make money, tell a great story, or even sway the masses with their dazzling marketing or brand names.

What the business world especially needs are more who would operate with unswerving integrity, all the time, every time.

Most individuals can do the right thing when they're exposed or pushed in a corner like a rat in a trap. But that's not integrity. That's simply complying in the moment.

Integrity is doing the right thing *because* it's the right thing to do. That's the motivation. Not fear. Not duty. Not ego. But simply because it's *right*.

Heroic leaders act from a set of moral principles that provide a foundation for their lives. The fact is, if people can't count on you, as a leader, to do the right thing, they just won't be able to count on you at all.

> ***Integrity is doing the right thing because it's the right thing to do.***

Consistency will build and earn trust, and you won't have consistency without integrity. A weak leader will look for ways to opt out of the tough choices, but the heroic leader will be driven to the right thing and act on it every time, regardless of outside pressure.

It's not based on a feeling or a notion, but a sense of moral fortitude that, over time, develops a strong reputation of reliability and trustworthiness.

Trust and Tylenols. In 1982 seven people died as a result of poisoning of Tylenol pills in the Chicago area. This led to Johnson & Johnson halting production and recalling every bottle from every shelf. This was a decision that would cost the company an estimated 100 million dollars. While it could be viewed as a costly decision, the return of restored confidence and assurance in the product more than compensated. James Burke, the CEO at the time, was heard to say, *it's not hard to do the right thing when you know what the right thing is*. This demonstrated a heart of integrity that easily produced the right decision.

Leaders don't act on feelings. Intuition can be vague. Leaders act their way into a feeling, not feel their way into action. That's integrity. It's the concrete with which the foundation of trust will be laid.

How well do I do my job and generate success for my team? While character is crucial for building trust, competency is not far behind. Trust is not offered to those who can't do their job. Remember, trust is confidence. That includes knowing someone can perform their assigned task. We believe that when we board a plane the pilots have been properly trained to take off, fly, and land well. We believe the surgeon has been adequately schooled and trained to perform a successful operation, even with the inherent risks of surgery. We even believe the person cooking our meal at the restaurant won't poison us!

The people you lead will need to trust that you know what you're doing, are growing, and creating an environment for them to do the same. Heroic leaders grow and help everyone they lead do the same for greater success. They get the job done and strengthen this important element of the trust dynamic.

> *The people you lead will need to trust that you know what you're doing, are growing, and creating an environment for them to do the same.*

How big is my ego? Does it need "downsizing?" It's hard to follow someone with a big head (figuratively speaking).

Leadership is about serving others, not the reverse. It's not about *I* or *me*, but *us* and *we*.

Too many see it as the former and allow hubris to run away with their attitude and approach.

The best leaders are the humblest. Practice humility, which is not thinking less of yourself, but *thinking of yourself less*. (More about that in Chapter 9.)

Egos get in the way. They dominate and take up too much space in conversations and situations. Keep your ego in check and practice humility. While leadership *is* the determining factor for success or failure, don't let that go to your head. (See above.)

Do I treat people like human beings, or just tools to get the job done? Leaders treat people like the human beings they know them to be. Controllers treat the same as subjects, minions, or simply a means to an end.

Disrespect can erode trust in a cruel and unjust way. And no one will trust and follow a jerk. People are human, not machines. Compassion demonstrates that the leader knows that and treats them respectfully. (More about that, also, in Chapter 9.)

These elements not only validate the imperative of trust but can give you solid practices to instate. It *will* require more than a casual effort to construct. Earning trust calls for credible and accountable action to establish and grow. Is there a risk? Yes. But the prospect of more group success and stronger, supportive relationships is worth it.

Ultimately trust and unity are about people and what, together, a cohesive team can do far and above what they could separately.

Remember, *no one climbs the mountain alone.*

The Value of Trust

- Trust is foundational. Without it you have nothing.
- Trust and unity are tied, explicably, together.
- Trust is earned, not given.
- If you can't be counted on to do the right thing, you can't be counted on.
- Do your job. And help others do theirs successfully.
- Don't have a big head. It's not all about you.
- Treat others well. They're human beings, not subjects.

Chapter 4

THE PRICE OF PROWESS

Chapter 4
The Price of Prowess

You have to give up to go up
—John Maxwell.

Superheroes have it easy when it comes to their powers—the fictional ones, that is.

Whether it's being from another planet, having been struck by lightning, or bit by a radioactive spider, their powers are mostly accidental and not usually due to their own efforts (Batman being at least one exception).

Imagine having one or more of these astonishing abilities bestowed on you by some freak occurrence and the tremendous opportunity to do more for the world than you ever could have previously imagined.

But, alas, being able to fly, run through walls, or lift buildings still only exists in folklore and on the big screen, not the physical world in which we live.

But remember, the powers we're outlining in this book are for all of us mere mortals. Leadership is a skill. But not one for the upper echelon of humanity. It's an accessible skill that can be taught, learned, and developed. As such, it can absolutely still be heroic, extraordinary, and world changing.

No cape required.

Leadership is everything. Leaders set the tone. Leaders can make things happen on an exponential level. Leadership is not a place on an organizational chart, but a role that individuals are called to play that goes far beyond a corner office. It's not static. If you're not growing and learning, neither will those you seek to influence.

Indra Nooyi, CEO of PepsiCo, says it this way:

If you want to improve the organization, you have to improve yourself and the organization gets pulled up with you.

While leadership is not mystical or magical that cuts both ways. It's not easily or lazily expanded. There are truths about leadership that can't be ignored. Buying in to misnomers about how leadership is rightly defined is what has hampered would-be leaders for generations, as have some of the enduring myths that have become permanently etched in their thinking.

One popular myth says *leaders are born.*

A story is told of a traveler visiting a distant and remote village. During his walk, he approached an older gentleman sitting at a fountain. "Excuse me, sir. I'm wondering, have any great leaders been born here?"

"No", replied the old man. "Only babies."

Truth: We are *all* born babies. While mine is now 18, I know the two or three things babies know how to do when they're infants. Everything else is learned.

As one of the greatest football coaches of all time has said:

The Price of Prowess

Leaders are made, they are not born. They are made by hard effort, which is the price which all of us must pay to achieve any goal that is worthwhile—Vince Lombardi.

While some people may be more inclined to lead and possess greater potential than others, I don't believe great leaders are simply born that way. It's the same reason toddlers don't drive.

But everyone has certain *prowess* that can be refined to prove the kind of leader they will become. Growing and enlarging that capacity is essential to increase the potential good that can come from flourishing leadership.

That's heroic, and requires the same level of effort.

> **Leaders are made, not born**
> **—Vince Lombardi.**

As mentioned, leaders have an opportunity to affect an organization in exponential ways and in many key areas. These can include ...

Defining Culture. Make no mistake, every group and organization has one. When a certain number of employees behave a certain way, it creates a certain culture. And culture trumps everything. Culture, for any group, is what people believe and what they do as a result. It's *belief* and *behavior*. Leaders must stay aware and seek to shape the ethos of their organization lest it happen by default.

Mission Support. Leaders can (and should) articulate the mission, vision, and focus of the organization in a way that's unique to their position and will inspire the troops. Leadership should motivate, not deflate. The way leadership advocates the direction the team and organization should go will determine how enthusiastically they will travel down that road.

Demonstrating Passion. If 75% of employees are not engaged at work (according to Gallup) then some of the blame probably resides with leadership. Remember, leadership is everything and *impacts* everything. If you're not passionate about your work or your team and what they're doing, neither will they be. Passion and enthusiasm are contagious and make all the difference in celebrating, or enduring, work. Let people see why you're passionate about it!

Modeling Values. Values matter. Companies have values and people have values. Values indicate what's important. Thy dictate behavior. Values shape people and organizations in ways mere words won't. Values are *caught*, not taught. People are intensely more interested in what a leader does, based on his or her value system, than what is said. By virtue of choosing to be, or become, a leader, you are also choosing the part of role model. You don't get to opt out of that one. What is your team catching based on what you're exhibiting? What are the values that will make the greatest difference for your team?

Values are caught, not taught.

Working Relationships. While not every leader is highly relational, the importance of healthy relationships, and the ability to connect with people, can't be understated. Really, everything is relational. Winning with people, and helping others do the same, is a key test of leadership by creating the collaboration every successful organization needs. Relational capital is an investment always worth the venture.

Practicing Accountability. Success throws a party, but failure mourns alone. It's easy to puff one's chest out when things go well. It's also easy to point fingers when the reverse happens. Accountability is a coin with two sides. Holding others accountable is void and partial unless the leader does the same for self.

Having said that, we all have expectations. This is critical as it relates to accountability. Heroic leaders have elevated standards that are clear and clearly communicated. And when individuals fail to meet the bar, courageous leaders, who practice integrity, will hold themselves and their teams accountable for their actions and behavior. They will caringly correct (and self-correct) when necessary. Accountability is the acid test for any great leader.

Creating Change. The fact is change will happen on its own. The mantra *change is good* is too simplistic for worthy consideration. Change *can* be good, but often is severely hampered and disrupted depending on the amount of resistance returned by an individual or group. Some adopt early, some much later. Some, not at all. Picture a stick. Now picture that stick in a pool of mud. That's resistance.

Resistance is an actual force that seeks to oppose or cause a change to fail. The heroic leader will not only serve to be a positive catalyst for change but will not allow fear and assumption to prevent what change may do for the advancement of the mission.

Too often organizations are reactive, not initiative-taking. Change happens *to* them not *for* them. That's not leadership. Heroic leaders act as robust facilitators for change and challenge what has become comfortable. They help their team become change *resilient* and teach them to do more than simply reject something different out of hand.

Heroic leaders act as robust facilitators for change and challenge what has become comfortable.

Fostering Respect. As mentioned, part of leading is creating a safe and healthy place for people to coexist and be treated fairly and with respect. Esteem is deeply craved, though not as frequently, or freely, given to others. Just as with trust, teamwork, cooperation, and other key elements of a healthy community, respect is high on the same list. Heroic leaders champion the proper treatment of others, every day, through their caring communication and conduct.

While this is not an exhaustive list, it should be obvious that growing and developing one's prowess will raise the level and widen the scope of every emerging and seasoned leader. The further the progress, the more doors he or she can open of endless opportunities for those in their charge.

But all I need is charisma, right?

Another popular myth is that you must have a big, bombastic personality to be a leader. You need to be able to light up a room like a Bill Clinton or be effervescent in your speech or delivery.

Not true.

There are numerous examples of very effective leaders—like Calvin Coolidge, otherwise known as "Silent Cal" because he used few words—that easily dispels this myth.

Dwight Eisenhower and Harry Truman were not big personalities, but both helped win the Second World War, respectively.

Character will *always* be more important than charisma.

I can fake charisma (and probably have). Character is real. Charisma may create an impression for a moment; character creates a legacy of steady conduct that can live on for generations.

Character sits at the core of a successful leadership journey. Heroic leaders need a solid center from which to operate. Character is that basis.

> *Character will always be more important than charisma.*

Don't get stuck.

Measure of influence is determined by current degree of leadership. We all have a ceiling that doesn't, and shouldn't, remain permanent. Many never leave what could be described as entry level or positional.

Positions of management and leadership can be awarded so easily, often out of expedience. Imagine Joe is great at his job and has worked at the company for a while and is a faithful employee. So, we make him a supervisor.

Unfortunately, there's no silver bullet or magic wand that will instantly change him into a mature leader. There's no phone booth in which to jump. No fairy dust to sprinkle.

Joe has a plethora of new responsibilities and is still the same person he was before he was given his new role. Again, it's not like being struck by lightning and receiving some meta human ability. Leaders are made, but not like that.

Almost never does acquiring a title and position consequentially equal superlative leadership, or *any* kind of leadership for that matter. At least not at first.

Having a title makes you a *boss*. That's not necessarily bad, but it's too easy to just remain there: a boss with a title.

Truthfully, receiving a title doesn't require any great level of maturity, experience, or even qualifications. Anyone can be *given* one. How many people have operated under the guise that they were good leaders, when, in all actuality, they were just positional title holders? (And I don't mean title holder as in world champ.)

Having a title makes you a boss, not necessarily a leader.

There's a great danger in believing you have more advancement than you actually do. It can cause a wide variety of damage and personal destruction. Those who strand themselves on the entry level of leadership might remain for their entire career. Imagine the amount of people they churn and burn along the way. Think about those who have suffered under a person who never learned how to motivate properly, influence, and inspire, but rather likely had to resort to prodding, coercion, and control to wring the demanded results.

Remember, superpowers, and heroic leadership, should be used for good. It will be if the right ground is cultivated.

Admittedly, I write this as a recovering control freak.

Early in my career I believed I needed to monitor every aspect of whatever project or event was in process. Instead of appreciation from the team, I received more consternation and frustration.

You can't control people. You can try, but the only choice is between leadership or control. You can't have both, at least not without pushback from what will inevitably be an unhappy crew.

Managing vs. leading.

It's important to understand that there is a difference between managing and leading. One is not right and the other wrong, or one good and one bad. Both are needed and clarification helps establish the balance.

Managers focus on things, schedules, assignments, and whatever technical matters need to synchronize to move things along. Leaders focus on the team, casting vision, motivating, coaching, and cheering them on.

The result? To effectively square the two, one will manage the *process* but lead the *people*. To get that backwards is not only counterproductive but demoralizing and insulting.

People don't want to be managed; they want to be led.

When people feel they're being managed, or worse, micromanaged, they might feel like idiots who cannot be trusted with the task at hand. Leadership is about empowerment, and that doesn't happen without a good amount of authority given. Those who get stuck with the wrong understanding of the relationship between managing and leading are the ones who make terrible, or at best, mediocre bosses, never great leaders. Certainly not heroic ones.

You can lead people or try to control them. You can't do both.

Growing is not optional.

Why do some get stuck on entry level? Why do they not pass this initial phase? Why not proceed to higher summits and peaks?

A better question is why wouldn't a caring leader *want* to grow and develop into the best version of themselves and their potential? Could it be the spirit is willing, but the flesh is weak?

Complacency and laziness have likely prevented, and even forfeited, more personal and professional success than practically any other factor. Too often the approach is to put in the minimum effort and still expect maximum return. Life has a way of reminding you it doesn't work that way. Then entropy can take over and everything tied to a person's chance to grow simply settles to the lowest common denominator.

Minimum, or half effort, will get synonymous results.

Some want a steak for the price of a Happy Meal. While the cost of the latter has gone up, the point remains: there is a price to pay for increasing prowess.

Value perceived leads to value exchanged.

As you shop and pick up that item off the rack that strikes your fancy, you may quickly replace it once you've looked at the price tag. Did the desire for the item change? Probably not. More likely the unwillingness to pay what is now perceived as too high a price has lessened that desire.

Instantly it can become an issue of diminished returns in view of the expense. The *juice* has to be worth the *squeeze*.

The bigger the prize, the stronger the pursuit. Heroic leaders recognize the potential for impacting and empowering others is too great a reward to waste away in the desolate land of complacency. Heroic leaders happily take the steps to pursue the ongoing journey of their own evolution.

Heroic leaders don't become that way by relying on casual commitment. Really those two words don't even go together. There's nothing casual about the price of prowess.

> *Minimum, or half efforts, will get synonymous results.*

Leaders don't drift up, they step up.

The climb can be laborious and often tedious, but the lessons and instruction, found in the feet and inches, are more than worth the effort.

Heroic leaders assume a posture of life-long learning and are their best advocates when it comes to continuous improvement. Remember vision, that snapshot, or image, of a preferable future. No one should be the same person they were five years ago and should not be the same five years from now.

Lethargy can creep in for anyone, at any time, and take hold. Heroic leaders, those who want to rise to each occasion and challenge, will steel themselves and pay whatever price necessary to grow their prowess.

These are the heroes we remember; the ones you and I read about and honor.

We don't remember those who never grew. Others may. Those who had the misfortune of working for a poor boss and must reflect painfully on those days wondering why that person never chose to mature past the point of simply telling people what to do.

Some circumstances may be specific, but the general cause remains the same.

Upward mobility costs. And many are just not willing to pay.

From dropout to Founding Father.

Benjamin Franklin never made it out of the sixth grade. Still, he became one of the greatest intellectuals of his day as well as an entrepreneur, statesmen, and ambassador for the burgeoning United States of America.

His exit from formal education was not by choice. His subsequent commitment to self-education, however, was. He began receiving such learning from constant reading and absorbing information on a host of topics while working at his brother's print shop.

Franklin even formed a library for artisans and others to trade books and learn from each other.

While dropping out of school is not advisable, Franklin easily proved the potential of plotting your own path to personal and professional advancement. (Wow, that was almost a tongue twister.)

We don't remember those who never grew.

It should be obvious that while *desire* is a key element in increasing one's aptitude as a leader, that will matter little if there is not convincing, and often massive action.

Taking Driver's Ed (which I hated) would have largely been a waste had I never actually gotten behind the wheel. Of course, for some drivers, it doesn't look like it did much good anyway.

Leadership is not passive. Action is the great separator. There are what can best be described as key *activators* that can serve to encourage and energize the quest for growth on which every leader should embark.

The dictionary (yes, dictionary) defines the term *activator* as *a substance that stimulates or initiates a chemical process*. And while I didn't take chemistry in high school, I get the idea. Leadership will benefit from a constant, gentle agitation so that dormancy doesn't emerge.

Employing the following with enthusiasm and fervor will help ensure that the you that starts this journey will not be the same one at the end.

Challenge your competency.

Are you competent? Yes. Everyone is a "10" somewhere (but not everywhere).

As mentioned in the previous chapter, competency is simply knowing and being able to perform that which you've been assigned, your job. This is just one reason people will follow you.

But you can't rest there. Camping out at a certain level is derelict, and standing still is a myth. You're actually wafting backwards as time is lurching forward. The moment you finally realize the drift, a great deal of opportunity has already been lost and others have passed you by.

Resting on your laurels?

In Ancient Greece laurel wreaths were given as a symbol of status or success. A "laureate" was someone so crowned with the leafy headwear.

You can almost picture awardees walking with pride as they displayed their wares and markings of achievement. One we would imagine as well deserved.

While the phrase "resting on his laurels" is not accurate as it relates to this origin, the lesson still applies; resting, camping, stalling, slacking: none of these are friends to the challenging of one's competency.

Camping out at a certain level is derelict and standing still is a myth.

Don't posterize your talent, amplify it!

A struggling sales rep entered his manager's office, exasperated after several days of failing to make a single sale. He felt defeated and clearly discouraged.

"I don't understand it, boss. I can't catch a break! It doesn't make sense. I've had 25 years of sales experience and I'm still failing."

The manager paused for a moment and gently, but emphatically, said, "No, you've had one year of sales experience *25 times*."

Time served can simply equal tenure if competency is not challenged and augmented. Consider what you are doing, today, in this moment, and continuously, to get better and *be* better. Guard against complacency. What war are you fighting, in your mind, to keep your eyes looking ahead to that improved you that's just ahead in the distance?

Find a coach.

Everyone needs a coach. Everyone should *be* a coach. Learning from your own experience, including all the successes and mistakes, certainly has immeasurable value. But a lot of grief and heartache can be saved by learning from someone who's already been there, done that, got the T-Shirt, and the coffee mug.

Even Tiger Woods has a coach.

Having a coach doesn't mean you're admitting a position of weakness, but one of strength, though we are all a mixed bag of both.

Coaches can lift you to a higher plane with a hand up while maintaining respect for the strides you've already made. A good coach will mix teaching, inspiration, and caring correction to lead you to that next stage. From the sideline or the dugout, or in the context of a mentoring relationship, an observant coach can see things you can't.

What a coach can see:

- ➢ *Bad form:* You may be performing or behaving incorrectly and have been doing so for a long period of time. That will only become more permanent if not remedied.

Sometimes you and I just need someone to tell us, "You're doing it wrong."

- *Potential roadblocks or potholes.* If your coach has already made the journey to where you're headed, he or she knows where the hazards are. They know what dangers lie ahead and can give fair warning. Better to be aware and in advance to easily bypass them. Why waste time in a trap that could have been avoided? Coaches will spare you that grief.

- *Blind spots.* Read this twice: *we all have blind spots*. Bad things can happen on the road if you start to move or swerve into the other lane without looking to see the vehicle beside you. There's a similar danger to not noticing the object that's about to crash into your person because you can't (or won't) acknowledge it, or are simply unaware. A loving coach won't shy away from pointing out perilous blind spots so they can be brought into the light and rectified.

- *Suggested improvements.* Coaches don't simply criticize. Anyone can do that. They provide both instruction and insight to prompt greater effectiveness and performance. Criticism tends to be a detracting end in itself. Little is required to only point out what someone is doing wrong. But versed coaches are wise enough to use mistakes and inadequacies as teaching moments and opportunities to offer guidance and support for how to best move forward.

Find a coach. Choose wisely and receive all the wisdom he or she can offer.

> *Sometimes you and I just need someone to tell us, "You're doing it wrong."*

Make mistakes.

Okay, this one may not be too difficult to pull off. One doesn't actually need to *try* to make mistakes. They happen naturally as part of the human experience.

But part of the growth barrier that many individuals face is the abject fear of failure—the possibility that the success hoped for falls short. Embarrassment and disappointment ensues.

As John Kennedy stated:

Victory has a thousand fathers, but defeat is an orphan.

It can be a lonesome experience to err and blunder when all the fingers are pointing at you. A common myth of leadership is that the person out in front is void of the prospect of tripping and falling as he or she marches ahead.

We *all* stumble and tumble. Failure and mistakes are as common and normal as the sun rising and setting.

Truman Capote said it this way:

Failure is the condiment that gives success its flavor.

Mistakes can be great allies in the journey of self-discovery and learning, as they will teach you much more than your successes. It's natural to want to spurn missteps or setbacks, as they may seem to slightly smudge the veneer that has been created (perhaps more in one's own mind). But the leader who can extract every possible helpful lesson from transitory letdowns will come to appreciate their visits, not candidly expel them. Mistakes can give us invaluable introspective peeks into ourselves, our humility, our teachability, and maturity quotient.

Welcome your mistakes as friends. Listen to what they have to say. They are wonderful teachers.

Invest your life.

Remember, there is a cost. Growth is not free or cheap. There is a price to pay, but the better term is *investment*.

Everyone gets three choices with what to do with their life: *waste* it, *spend* it, or *invest* it.

Lots of people waste their lives with trivial pursuits, coasting, and never reaching their full potential. Others *spend* their lives climbing the ladder of success, some stepping on people along the way, in pursuit of reaching an imagined summit or *castle in the sky*.

While there's nothing wrong with honest success, significance is a more meaningful pursuit for heroic leaders. Realizing that I'm not truly successful until someone else is, or we together, will prompt me to *invest* my life, not just spend it. And certainly not waste it!

> *Everyone gets three choices with what to do with their life: waste it, spend it, or invest it.*

Investment presumes a return. How much is regulated by amount. How much time are you devoting to reading, listening to other leaders, thinking, planning, setting goals, taking deliberate steps of focus for your own development as a leader and individual?

Time is a resource. The clock will tick away and become an evil bandit without a sense of purposeful time leadership. Invest in yourself so you can more profitably do the same for those you seek to lead. The returns can be immeasurable and timeless.

It costs something to go up, to grow as a leader. Heroic leaders aren't lazy or complacent. They train. They work hard. They recognize skill is important but can be, and *must* be, developed.

The leadership journey is not a fairy tale. It's real and no lightning bolt is coming.

There is a price for the investment to be made, but the potential returns can be immeasurable.

Don't be afraid to pay the price. Cultivate your prowess.

The Price of Prowess

* Everyone can become and grow as a leader.
* To go up you have to give up.
* Leaders are not born. Babies are.
* Character is more important than charisma.
* Manage the process. Lead the people.
* Grow your competency. Don't get stuck.
* Get a coach.
* Make mistakes your friends. They have a lot to say.
* Invest your life, don't waste it.

Chapter 5

THE PASSION OF A JUST CAUSE

Chapter 5
The Passion of a Just Cause

> *We always have to be in the middle of the action 'cause we're the warriors. And without some challenge, without some ... war to fight, then the warrior might as well be dead*
> —Apollo Creed (*Rocky IV*).

In every hero's story there's always a motive to fight. Heroes battle for a reason. They battle for a *cause*. Whatever the adversary or mission, deep down they believe their cause is just, and that's part of what makes them heroes.

Why we enjoy reading about and celebrating these champions of right, in the first place, is the underpinning of something bigger than themselves for which they strap on their costumes and live to save the day.

Of course, by now you should know that no mask and spandex are required to discover and work for a purpose and mission that is honorable and righteous.

Everyone needs a cause. Everyone needs a calling bigger than self, a passion that will not only energize their life but change someone else's. Without it, the sense of merely existing takes hold and one simply takes up space until the end.

When I was in graduate school, one of the assignments was an essay regarding the words we wanted on our tombstone. Now, while that sounded a bit morbid to think about, the idea was centered around what the instructor referred to as our *ultimate contribution*.

This was the first time I'd heard that term, but it stuck. How did I want to contribute to the world, society, and future generations, that would be worthy of this gift we call life?

The heroic leader will inspire others to move beyond mere existence and into a meaningful cause. The difference between the two can't be understated.

How many people do you know go through life making what's known as a first-class commitment to what, ultimately, proves to be a second-class cause?

Not enough are driven by a strong sense of mission, purpose, or a reason that produces a call that must be answered with enthusiasm and passion on a daily basis.

While each life has a definite purpose, causes can be presented at various times in alignment with one's mission and calling.

Every life is a story waiting to be told. A great commitment to a great cause will build a great life and speak volumes to the world about who you are, what you believe, and the difference you want to make.

Every life is a story waiting to be told.

A clarion call.

At a time when a strong and fervent voice was needed, in the face of societal racial injustice, Martin Luther King, Jr. proved the worth of a life wholly committed to a just cause.

The Passion of a Just Cause

Standing on the steps of the Lincoln Memorial, in the brutal August heat, this Southern Baptist preacher turned activist fervently sounded the battle cry to fight for an envisioned world of equality and opportunity for all, regardless of race or creed.

Referred to as his most remembered and excitable speech, King implored America to abandon its biased treatment of those termed as *colored people* and promote unity for all.

Here are some of those historic words:

I have a dream that one day this nation will rise up and live out the true meaning of its creed: "We hold these truths to be self-evident: that all men are created equal."

I have a dream that one day on the red hills of Georgia the sons of former slaves and the sons of former slave owners will be able to sit down together at the table of brotherhood.

I have a dream that one day even the state of Mississippi, a state sweltering with the heat of injustice, sweltering with the heat of oppression, will be transformed into an oasis of freedom and justice.

I have a dream that my four little children will one day live in a nation where they will not be judged by the color of their skin but by the content of their character.

I have a dream today.

I have a dream that one day, down in Alabama, with its vicious racists, with its governor having his lips dripping with the words of interposition and nullification; one day right there in Alabama, little black boys and black girls will be able to join hands with little white boys and white girls as sisters and brothers.

I have a dream today.

I have a dream that one day every valley shall be exalted, every hill and mountain shall be made low, the rough places will be made plain, and the crooked places will be made straight, and the glory of the Lord shall be revealed, and all flesh shall see it together.

Dr. King's words still echo today. This is because they were more than just nice phrases in a public address. What Martin Luther King, Jr. was saying represented hope for an entire race of people as well as the whole of America, even if some couldn't see it at the time.

Ideas come and go, even good ones. This was not that. This was not a fad or passing fancy. Martin Luther King passionately lived his commitment to what he believed was a *just cause*, ultimately dying at the hands of an assassin's bullet. Prior to that, he became the de facto leader of the Civil Rights Movement that became a force in the 1960s and has reverberated ever since. While he and many others rallied to fight for this cause, it was done peaceably and without violence—a stark contrast to the way many of his followers, and those he was seeking to help, were cruelly treated.

King himself was harassed, threatened, and arrested 30 times. He put his fellow activists at risk, telling them to protest, but to do so without aggression. During the Montgomery Bus Boycott, which lasted for 385 days, King's house was bombed, and he and his family were constantly threatened. Still, he soldiered on. Why?

In the face of constant danger and incarceration, why did King continue to challenge what was seemingly overwhelming and often oppressive opposition to his campaign?

Because he believed cause was just. It *was* right. It was pure and worth any risk.

MLK proved that during his life and in his death. That's the power of conviction that drives a just and worthy cause.

Everyone has thoughts and opinions.

You can find a barrage of them on social media, in the break room, or around the water cooler. While people may argue, ad nauseum, over the pet opinions, they likely wouldn't die to support them. Only convictions deserve that kind of commitment and ultimate sacrifice. This is why a cause greater than self is grounded in conviction. You have to be prepared to not only commit your life, but be prepared to lose it, if called upon, for what you believe. Great causes and deep convictions are worth dying for.

Conviction that birthed a nation.

Declaring independence from a radical king was a profound and radical act. To fight and bleed for that freedom was another brand of heroism that has carved our founders' names in the annals of America's history forever.

While many had a role to play in the founding of America, those who actually signed the document and listed their names at the bottom of the Declaration of Independence were doing so under the backdrop of probable and severe retaliation.

This would prove prophetic, as many suffered retribution at the hands of the British.

There were five that were captured and tortured. Twelve had their homes burned. Others lost their sons in the war. Still others suffered further loss due to attacks by the military as well as looters.

These men sacrificed their own lives, and those of their families, not for a whimsical idea, but one of the most shining examples of a just cause: freedom.

This is the kind of conviction that will help every individual to tell their best and greatest story.

We're all given talents, gifts, and abilities to be used and, too often, those wonderful gifts sit on a shelf or are misdirected. The world never gets to truly benefit from what we have to offer.

Some stories are never told. How many campaigns have died simply from lack of inclination and the willingness to step out and be used?

History records the ones who saw a need and responded in a way that was disruptive and history altering, like Martin Luther King, Jr.

A more ancient example would be the story of Nehemiah, from the Old Testament.

> Great causes and deep convictions are worth dying for.

Switching careers. Answering the call.

In ancient times an individual by the name of Nehemiah answered a call and made a difference. A cupbearer by trade, he stepped out of his comfort zone to lead the effort to rebuild temple walls in Jerusalem that had been in disrepair for 142 years following Babylonian exile.

Walls were especially important in those days because that's how cities protected themselves. Without them they were defenseless. They were vulnerable to attack. When an army went to take over a city, that was the first thing they would seek and destroy.

In Nehemiah's mind the walls had simply been down too long. Something needed to be done. Someone needed to rise and accept the challenge. Nehemiah asked for permission to return with a group and rebuild. That's where Nehemiah's best story begins.

Clearly it would have been easier for Nehemiah to hear about this situation and simply choose to ignore it as he was contently working as a cupbearer for the king, which was a mostly cushy job. But when you recognize a need, and it moves you, you can't sit still. You must take up the cause. Or maybe the cause takes you.

Nehemiah was not only aware of the need, but he also responded in a way that showed genuine concern, deep enough to move him to pray, fast, and mourn, ultimately for months before taking action.

If the walls were down for 142 years, clearly other people knew about it. But they also proved they didn't care enough to do anything about it. Nehemiah *did*.

While Nehemiah was not a builder, he was able to rally many together, and despite distractions, defamation, and even danger, they were able to get the project completed in a record time of 52 days! All because he saw a need and responded in practical, yet powerful, ways.

The greatest endeavors and causes can be birthed by a resolute choice to move out of your comfort zone, into the unknown, and be used in amazing and astounding ways.

And if you can rally people to your cause, as both MLK and Nehemiah were able to do, that's true, *heroic* leadership.

People are looking for a cause. Heroic leaders provide that. They rise above the mediocrity of what I call the driftwood life that simply floats with whatever wave is the strongest.

Anyone can do that. Many do.

Heroic leadership is purposeful, not accidental. It's certainly not lazy or apathetic. A just cause will inspire a leader to move from the ordinary into the extraordinary, and help others do the same, not as a grandiose gesture for self-gratification or ego, but simply for the greater good that will result.

 *People are looking for a cause. Heroic leaders provide that.*

As Steve Goodier states:

Causes do matter. And the world is changed by people who care deeply about causes—about things that matter. We don't have to be particularly smart or talented. We don't need a lot of money or education. All we really need is to be passionate about something important; something bigger than ourselves. And it's that commitment to a worthwhile cause that changes the world.

The dedication and commitment necessary to live for a just cause are too high for a laissez-faire approach to respond to the needs that require a champion. And, looking at the current landscape, there are more blights than lights. Any and every life can shine and dispel some of that darkness.

Moving towards a cause.

The average number of moves in a chess game is around 40. If I were playing, that number would be far less, based on my poor skill level. Having said that, even I know the most important move is the first one.

Making a deliberate, purposeful move is part of what separates those who almost did something from those who actually did. No one will remember what you only *thought* about doing.

Heroic leaders step out and make brave moves for a cause they believe is just.

Here's how:

Respond to a need.

If only partially aware, no one would honestly be able to argue that there are needs all around them. There are injustices that must be corrected, wrongs to be righted, or something lost that must be restored. The first step is to not only acknowledge that a need exists. That's too easy. All that's required for that is a reasonable power of observation and perception.

The potential spark begins by asking the question as to what should be done about it, and whether *you* should be the one to answer the call. And if so, *will* you answer?

The heroes we celebrate in the pages of action stories never seemed to hesitate. (Not the ones I remember, anyway.)

The tragedy can be that all the goodness and history-changing prospect is lost in vacillation. The shrugging of the shoulders, fuzzy indecision, or standard waffling can prove to be a death knell to any worthy campaign before it's ever begun. Merely saying "Not my problem" can feel painless, but abdication and valiant effort are rarely, if ever, synonymous.

Responding to a need is a courageous choice to move from the sidelines on to the field, from a spectator to a participator. Spectators enjoy more respite, but participators know the joy and satisfaction of a life well lived for others.

Again, people are looking for someone to champion their cause. Responding to that cry, and those needs, is the first step in discovering a passionate life of purpose.

Move from the known into the unknown.

This is where a lot of people may opt out. Even if they recognize a need and a worthy battle to wage, it's way too comfortable on this side of the arena. People like the comfort zones so carefully designed and built. But remember, a great commitment to a great cause can build a great life. This involves change and tackling the fear of the unknown.

Personally, I like history, not mystery. Not knowing what will happen in a story is tantalizing for some, but frustrating for me. I'd rather know what *already* happened, not what *may* happen.

However, to truly experience the passion of a great and just cause, what may seem mysterious on this side of the decision must be face daringly, though not foolishly, and navigated.

It's only unknown until you get there.

Martin Luther King's known world was preaching, not social activism. Nehemiah's known world was taste testing, not construction.

But travel to the unknown they did, and the results speak for themselves.

They did not do so blindly. Eyes wide open, and with much planning and preparation, they turned the mystery into history with informed, but bold, action.

 *It's only unknown until you get there.*

Stay committed.

This is why a casual commitment to a worthy and just cause simply won't do. If the *why* is not strong enough, it will be too easy to quit when adversity or disappointment comes. And it *will* come.

I remember during one of our ventures unloading a trailer full of portable equipment in the summer heat. I was mumbling and grumbling about the fact that no one had showed and, technically, I had other responsibilities than this.

But I was reminded that a fleeting moment of frustration shouldn't be enough to dampen the commitment to the reason behind something even as mundane as grunt work. This sentiment helped me in times of personal attacks and opposition, as I was forced to mentally, and sometimes verbally, evoke the original call that I chose to answer and, thus, carry on. Commitment is key because the opposition will come. No leader that has accomplished much can honestly say they have suffered little. Whether through adverse circumstances, critics, fatigue, or failure, a vow to stay committed to the end will always be tested.

But the greater the test, and the more tests that are passed, the greater the story. If the heroes mentioned in this chapter could persevere in the face of death, there's more than enough motivation for the courageous leader of today.

The Passion of a Just Cause

Find a wall (a cause), find your tribe, and make a change in the world that could last for generations.

Make your move and let your story be told.

- Every life is a story waiting to be told.
- A great commitment to a great cause will build a great life.
- Convictions are worth dying for.
- No one will remember what you thought about doing.
- Seeing the needs is not enough. Take action. Step out.
- Turn your mystery into history.
- Persevere and pass the test.
- Find your wall. Tell your story.

Chapter 6

THE REALITY OF HOPE

Chapter 6
The Reality of Hope

Hope is the thing with feathers that perches in the soul and sings the tune without the words and never stops at all
—Emily Dickinson.

Imagine temperatures so cold you could literally hear the water freeze. Your sleeping bag is basically a sheet of ice. You're incredibly hungry, as the last thing you ate was barely enough for the dogs you pray you won't have to sacrifice due to an ever-decreasing food supply.

All this while marooned 1,200 miles from any civilization.

Stranded. Shipwrecked on a barren winter land, completely separated from anyone who would even know you're there, all but eliminating the possibility that there would ever be a rescue.

These were the extreme, harsh conditions in which the crew of the *Endurance* found themselves during a failed expedition to the South Pole. The captain, Ernest Shackleton, led 27 men (plus a stowaway) on a journey to explore that bottom region of the world, only to have it upended by the worst that circumstance and nature had to offer.

Granted, these ventures were arduous enough. Though when the advertisement was placed for crewmembers, over 500 applied.

Here was the posting:

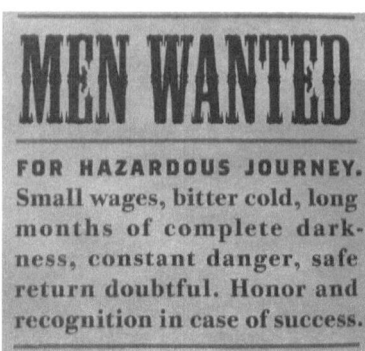

Clearly, Shackleton already knew, as did those who agreed to join him and his mission, there would be a distinct possibility, perhaps likelihood, of danger or even death.

That certainly became the case for the *Endurance* (a fitting name, by the way).

While crossing the Weddell Sea, not long after their departure, the ship encountered ice that, ultimately, they would not be able to escape. Normal protocol would be to simply wait until there was enough melting and breakage to continue. Unfortunately, that did not happen. In fact, after several weeks of poking and prodding through small openings in the ice, movement stopped and Shackleton and his men then waited 10 months for the ice to give way. It was all in vain. Worse, the drift of the ice was pushing them further away from what would have been a day's journey to a landing place. They were trapped and powerless to stop the backward flow.

The frozen water became a relentless snare that would not let go. In the words of one of the crew the ship was "frozen like an almond in the middle of a chocolate bar."

Waiting did not mean the members of the *Endurance* were docile. Hope is not passive. Recognizing the ice was slowly imploding the ship, Shackleton and his crew prepared for the arduous undertaking of living on the ice, gathering as many provisions as they could. The original idea was to walk across the *floe* (the sheet of ice) but given the men could only traverse a little over seven miles per day, that plan was discarded and replaced with that of accepting that they would need to live on the ice until conditions could improve.

Consider the amount of hope needed to face just that bitter prospect, especially without knowing for how long and if, not when, they would ever be saved. The time ultimately spent on this bed of ice would be 497 days. For over 16 months these men lived, worked, and slept on the arctic ground until it finally gave way, and they were free to launch their boats headed for land.

Imagine after almost a year and a half of life on a giant sheet of ice, now having to withstand an open ocean throwing glacial wind and waves in your face. Your boat battered for days, battling seasickness and dysentery for six days until you, mercifully, reach Elephant Island and dry land.

Given that the chances anyone finding them were very remote due to their location, Shackleton would eventually initiate their rescue taking five others, including Worsley, to sail to a whaling station over 800 miles away.

> *Hope is not passive.*

Consider the tremendous leadership that was employed, during their exile, to not allow, understandably, a deep sense of sorrow and despair to set in and become entrenched.

Part of Shackleton's genius was to keep his men active and focused on what they *could* control, not on what they *couldn't*. Faced with circumstances that would crush the average person, he staunchly decided to let positive action keep the embers of hope burning.

Heroic leadership is easy when conditions are favorable and warm. The plight of the *Endurance* was, literally, the extreme, polar opposite of that.

There's much more to this story. Many books have been written about what could easily sound like a Hollywood movie. But this was very real. These men were placed in the worst-case scenario possible. The presence of hope, and how this brave crew survived should, by no means, diminish the level of adversity and setbacks these men nobly faced, including the loss of Shackleton's beloved *Endurance*.

Consider what would go through a captain's mind as he was forced to watch his ship implode before his very eyes.

That alone could be cause for despair. But, throughout the entire ordeal, it was said of the seasoned explorer:

The Reality of Hope

Shackleton's spirits were wonderfully irrepressible considering the heartbreaking reverses he has had to put up with and the frustration of all his hopes for this year at least. One would think he had never a care on his mind & he is the life & soul of half the skylarking and fooling in the ship.

That's the kind of outlook the reality of hope can bring. Hope is not blind optimism or wishful thinking. Hope does not equal fallacy. It doesn't deny experience or pretend problems don't exist. Shackleton's actuality grimly greeted him and his men every day of their involuntary exile. Yet he found ways to keep the men together, support each other, and even laugh. They threw nightly parties, sang, entertained, and lifted each other when it would have been easier to descend downward into a state of utter misery.

They used hope to, quite literally, stay alive. It's that essential.

You can survive 40 days without food, three days without water, and eight minutes without air. But you can't honestly survive a single second without hope.

Dr. Emil Brunner said:

What oxygen is for the lungs, such is hope for the meaning of human life. Take oxygen away and death occurs through suffocation, take hope away and humanity is constricted through lack of breath; despair and hopelessness set in.

Hope is as vital as the air we breathe. Without it, life becomes an exercise in finding as many ways as possible to *cope* or just get by. People no longer *thrive*, they merely *survive*.

> *You can't survive a second without hope.*

While it's true that most of us will likely never have to do life on what was essentially a massive expanse of ice, the analogy still fits; it can certainly get cold from time to time. Hope doesn't deny that. Hope reinforces the mettle necessary to face it. Again, and again. And then *again*.

That's what the crew of the *Endurance* was able to do. What choice did they have? Where else could their minds go? Hope or despair. Possibility or predicament. Live or die.

They chose hope. They chose what would help them reconcile a harsh, unwanted, and potentially deadly predicament. Certainly, we don't know every thought that went through the minds of the crew. I'm sure some doubt crept in from time to time.

But the steady and positive leadership of the captain they would grow to view as a father figure helped allay those moments of doubt. He would help them, instead, experience days of what could be described as *constructive courage*.

What similar lessons can you or any leader apply to help a team live more optimistically with the reality of hope instead of the drain of adverse circumstances?

Keep your team distracted with work.

Now you and I both know that work is not (or shouldn't be) a *distraction*. It's the reason. It's the job! Often employees are distracted *at* work instead of *with* work. Thoughts of personal problems with the kids, the boyfriend, a sticky divorce, or other similar situations can often top the list of what people talk about at work.

While I think it's important for employees to know their boss and team cares, focusing too much time and attention on circumstances outside of the workplace can be the kind of distraction that will prove too diverting. Helping team members practice proper balance, which means finding success in both your personal and professional life, will help them stay actively focused.

Shackleton knew that left alone, and idle too long, the men's thoughts and emotions could drift to a place that wasn't positive or beneficial. Negative thoughts can easily slink into an empty or unoccupied mind. Shackleton kept his crew busy with activity and specific jobs, right down to washing and drying their socks, to keep them engaged and productive.

Heroic leaders stress the same kind of focus while, at the same time, not minimizing life's ups and downs. It can be a fine line to walk, but necessary to keep a group single-minded.

Don't forget to celebrate.

Even marooned on an icy wasteland, the crew of the *Endurance* found many ways to celebrate. Whether on Christmas, birthdays, and even dogsledding races, this kept morale high and promoted a cheerier sense of community and festivity. This spirit shone brightly in contrast to what was otherwise a dark time.

Celebration is an important part of life experience. Beyond birthdays and holidays, we give trophies and medals to competitors and athletes to acknowledge their victories as part of commemorating and honoring their achievement. It demonstrates that we care they won.

It should be no different for your team. Whether or not you hand out actual trophies or medals, free doughnuts, gift cards to Starbucks, or steak dinners, wins should be celebrated.

This kind of spirit keeps hope alive. A losing attitude can be assuaged, in part, by thoughtfully commemorating when a team or individual triumphs.

"No news is good news" is just weak and pathetic.

I remember early in my first leadership position having to request evaluation meetings with the board of directors so I could gauge how I, and my team, were performing.

I was often told, "If you don't hear anything from us, that means you're doing a good job."

Even I knew at a young age that's not how it should work. Internal victories are not enough. And public praise can be more valuable and motivational than one might think. When goodness happens throw a party! Shout it from the rooftops!

Feed the spirit of hope with celebration.

The Reality of Hope

> *Internal victories are not enough.*
> *When goodness happens, throw a party!*

Help your team lean on each other.

As mentioned in Chapter 3, unity matters, and in all seasons and situations. Union can be tested on a small scale as well as a large one. The magnitude to which the crew of the *Endurance* was tested would have to be described as no less than epic.

In a situation where it could have been just as easy to say, "Every man for himself," they chose to take the approach of every man for every *other* man. It was support each other or face the prospect of *burying* each other.

From football games during the day to singalongs at night, Shackleton provided opportunities for the men to demonstrate their care and guardianship of every other crew member.

One powerful instance of this kind of support came when the First Officer's (Greenstreet) milk accidentally spilled while he was caught in the middle of a scuffle. (I never said there weren't *some* moments of tension.)

You can imagine, as the crew was facing the dim prospect of starvation, the horror of seeing a vital sustenance like milk empty to the ground. After that moment passed, as well as some tears that flowed, one by one each man reached over and poured some of his own milk into Greenstreet's jug.

Think about what that sacrificial act by every crew member did for not only the distraught officer, but for the sense of solidarity. Heroic leaders will promote the same devotion and mutual concern. There's no room for personal agendas. We all need each other. Even Lone Ranger had Tonto. The truly close-knit will prove that by their fidelity to *all*.

Team unity, community, and group identity are all part of the high test for any leader. A test Shackleton passed brilliantly time and time again.

Actions like keeping the sleds together during marches and the tents close once on Patience Camp showed that the *Endurance* knew they were "in this together" in more than just name only. That's what kept hope alive and, in turn, each of those crew members during that fateful season.

Remember the mission.

While the expedition and journey were rudely interrupted, the original idea and mission could still prove to be a source of motivation. How easy it would have been for any of the crew members to quit. How simple, and perhaps understandable, would it have been to resign, leave, abandon not only hope, but their team, and everything they once stood for.

People do it every day. And way too easily.

When the pain of adverse circumstance overcomes hope, and why we're working this hard in the first place, resignation crawls in and people tend to check out. How many conversations have you had with team members who are still working but you suspect have resigned in place? They've forgotten the power of vision and the sense of mission. They've lost hope.

Overwhelm, stress, fear, anxiety, and despondency can be almost daily mixed with the other emotions like happiness, cheer, buoyancy, and spirit of optimism. Sometimes we have to swallow the bitter taste of defeat or hardship.

At the time of this writing, the entire planet is still reeling from impact of the COVID pandemic and the similar feelings *all* of us have experienced as businesses were shuttered, employees were sent home, and people were forced to isolate. And, of course, the deaths. Officially, the number of those is around 5,000,000.

It would take a lot of words and many, many more pages to attempt to describe the despair and despondency that millions and millions of people have endured over the past 18 months or more. From losing family members and friends, along with the opportunity to visit a hospital room or attend a funeral, the personal toll of this historic virus goes beyond one's bleakest imagination.

To be stranded with people around you that you can't see or touch has been a challenge not everyone was able to bear.

For businesses who were able to pivot and sustain throughout the crisis, *remembering the mission* and remaining committed to it, much like Shackleton and his crew, provided hope in the midst of severe hardship that has yet to completely yield.

When the pain of adverse circumstance overcomes hope, and why we're working this hard in the first place, resignation crawls in and people tend to check out.

Trying times are no time to quit trying. Hope can't be taken from you. It has to be surrendered.

Remind your team of the mission and let that translate into tangible and constructive courage.

That's the power and opportunity of leadership. That's the hope of heroic leadership.

Every leader can authentically present the reality of hope that will spur their team forward despite, and even because of, hard seasons.

What will you do to keep hope alive in the hearts and minds of those you lead?

When you think about quitting, remember the reason you started. Help your team do the same and keep alive the breath of hope.

- Hope is essential. It's the air we breathe.
- Hope does not deny the existence of challenges or difficulties but spurs one forward despite the adversity.
- Hope and positive action work hand in hand.
- Stay focused. Keep your mind on task.
- Don't forget to celebrate. Internal victories are not enough.
- Practice healthy community. We need each other.
- Remember the mission.

Chapter 7

Chapter 7
The Honor of Fighting Fair

An eye for an eye will only make the whole world blind
—Mahatma Gandhi.

Growing up, from the age of eight, I would find high adventure in the pages of comic books. In full color and rich dialogue (sometimes campy) heroes and villains would battle in stilled action that seemed to leap from every page and panel.

There was always a fight. Conflict was not only part of the story, it *was* the story. In elementary school we learned, when writing, that every story needs a protagonist and an antagonist, otherwise, there's little room for a plot or a compelling tale. Conflict is crucial to the narrative.

But while it's essential in fictional writing, conflict is something most seek to avoid in daily life.

Writers have the power of the pen to create an agreeable and worthy outcome, whereas those of us in the physical world don't always find it that simple and tidy. Either way, *conflict is inevitable*. It can't be avoided. When people attempt to, with a *head in the sand* approach, the conflict that predictably surfaces is exacerbated by a lack of preparedness and proactiveness.

If one knows conflict is unavoidable, then that fact alone should help one prepare and handle it in a way that doesn't damage relationships, morale, and the overall mission and success of the group. This happens all too often.

The typical manager spends 25–40% of his or her time dealing with workplace conflict. Another term for this is *putting out fires*. That's because when conflict happens, too many involved, and even uninvolved, are carrying around buckets of gasoline instead of buckets of water. This intensifies a situation and can cause it to quickly rage out of control.

Conflict doesn't have to burn this way. It doesn't have to rob a group or organization of so much life and energy. Conflict can actually be an important part of growth and a maturation process for individuals and a team. But, as with most leadership practices, it doesn't come easily or without care, forethought, and some degree of humility.

Conflict can make you *better* or *bitter*. Everyone gets to choose which. You know it's coming. Be ready when it does.

> *Conflict is inevitable.*
> *It can't be avoided.*

Before unpacking some of the best practices for resolving workplace conflict, it's worth noting that there are generally two types of conflict: *constructive* and *destructive*.

Obviously, any sensible leader would opt for an approach to conflict that protects others and builds, not destroys. Peek behind the curtains of a team that practices constructive conflict, and you will find individuals that do not shy away from disagreements, but will engage in debate that is not attacking, abrasive, rude, or whiny. While the phrase "disagree agreeably" sounds a bit cliché, it holds enough meaning and value to practice the overall principle.

Years ago while attending a conference one of the speakers mentioned the 85% rule. While I hate numbers (and math), this has stuck ever since.

The premise is that it would be fantasy to think that people who work and interact with each other on a daily basis will agree 100% of the time. I don't even agree with myself all the time, and likely you don't either. However, is it possible to agree on 85% of the big picture and what will keep a group together, fully functioning, learning, and growing?

That's the benefit of *constructive* conflict.

Why is it some would rather battle over the 15% of which they don't agree and leave the remaining 85% to wither away in the corner? Is it worth it to allow workplace conflicts to become personal and hateful over something that may or may not even affect the mission? Too many die on hills not worth the sacrifice. It happens all the time.

Constructive conflict will foster more discussion than destruction. The alternate choice, to attack, argue, isolate, and allow animosity to fester, will cause layers of dissention that could take years to peel away.

This doesn't have to be. You *can* fight fair.

Where is it written that people must point fingers and launch personal assaults when differences arise? Why is it that many are unable to separate the issue from the emotion they may feel steadily sliding to a bad place?

Heroic leaders help others understand the damage from reacting in a manner that is irresponsible and unhealthy. He or she must harness harmful behavior, or the results will reverberate, unrestrained until corrected. The signs will become obvious.

> *Conflict can make you better or bitter.*

What does it look like when individuals engage in destructive conflict? What are the symptoms?

- ➤ *Vindictive Behavior.* Sometimes people don't need to be right anymore, they just want to retaliate in an attempt to feel vindicated.

- ➤ *Blaming.* It's easier to shift blame and find fault in others.

- ➤ *Passive-Aggressive Communication.* The desire to control the situation with the unwillingness to be open, honest, and direct.

- ➤ *Personalizing.* Feelings get hurt and people tend to personalize matters (even when it's not).

- ➤ *Generalizing.* This happens when people use extreme terms like always and never. They go too far in their thinking and conversation.

- ➤ *Irrational Conduct.* Emotions take over reason. Behavior can become erratic and unpredictable, often with severe consequences, including the possibility of violence.

- ➤ *Demands and Ultimatums.* Lines in the sand are drawn and voiced. Ultimatums are a clear indication that a win-win solution is off the table. Demands are made that often include threats.

These are simply indications, not the *reasons* for rising tension. Very often symptoms are treated but not the disease. Thus, the carnage continues. If conflict need not be so destructive, then there must be a way to defuse it—truly *resolve* as opposed to simply *managing* it.

But before unpacking that it's important to see how escalation can happen more quickly than you may think.

All over a pig!

In 1878, Randolph McCoy accused Floyd Hatfield of stealing one of his hogs. This even went to trial, with Bill Staton as star witness. Staton sided with Hatfield and was later shot dead by Sam McCoy. All in all, 13 Hatfields and McCoys would eventually be killed before hostilities would subside. And if reports are true, all over a stolen pig?

While this is an extreme example, it demonstrates that conflict can rapidly intensify if not handled properly.

Regarding the *causes* of workplace conflict, and aside from the predictability of human nature, they can include:

➤ *Lack of common understanding*

➤ *Conflicting priorities/goals*

➤ *Lack of communication*

➤ *Unclear or unfair expectations*

➤ *Power plays*

The results of these are all counterproductive—competition, self-interest, win-lose attitude, and a closed, often siloed, environment. In a healthy work environment, the focus should be on *cooperation*, not *competition*. That can't happen when those lines of division get drawn.

If conflict has a chance to make a team stronger, instead of weaker, then it must be truly resolved. Issues don't go away by themselves or with the passage of time, even minor ones (that don't always remain minor).

Fair fighting is about working through critical issues together, finding common ground, and settling disputes with respect and civility. Have the conversation. The 800-pound gorilla will need to come out of the cage. He only grows angrier if he's denied.

Heroic leaders are assertive with their approach to conflict and help others process it with concern for others in mind. They demonstrate and advocate a desire and commitment to finding mutual solutions Otherwise, a conflict will *slide*.

Stages of a sliding conflict.

Again, conflict doesn't resolve itself and time is of the essence. *Time heals all wounds* is only partially true. Obviously, it's what you do with it. With passivity and inaction a situation can begin to deteriorate. This only makes it more difficult, the more time passes, to find a way out and truly move forward.

Here's how unresolved conflict slides:

Stage 1) Remedy. This is the initial stage that presents the best opportunity to resolve a particular issue. Granted, if heated arguments and verbal firebombs have already been launched, then sufficient time for heads to cool is needed. But waiting too long will start the dreaded skid.

The remedy stage, the early onset of conflict, is the ideal period when there can be rational recognition of a problem, belief it can be solved, commitment, and a plan to do so.

When that 800-pound gorilla is boldly let out of the cage, and the conversation takes place, the style of communication is key. *How* we say something is just as important as *what* we say. Issues will be resolved more productively, and in a healthy environment, if communication is assertive, not aggressive.

The remedy stage offers a prime opportunity to practice a **C.A.L.M.** conversation.

- **C:** Clarify the issue. Zero in on the problem, not a person. This should be the first question anytime conflict happens. Start the dialogue with, "What's the issue?" That way people can attack that together, not each other, and begin on the proper footing.

- **A:** Address the problem with the person. This is why assertive is the most effective style of communication. Why talk to other people about the situation instead of talking *to* the person? They are uninvolved and can do nothing to help remedy the situation. Those conversations are worthless and counterproductive.

- **L:** Listen. Most people, especially those in leadership, are great talkers. But you'll never hear or learn what you need to know by being the one who does all the talking.

- **M:** Make a plan to settle the issue. Unless a workable plan is created, and action taken, the issue is likely to reappear, repeatedly, at places and times where it can cause major upheaval.

Remedy to most any issue can be found if two or more people are willing to calmly talk, the sooner the better.

The 800-pound gorilla will need to come out of the cage. He only grows angrier if he's denied.

Repositioning. If resolution is not found quickly and successfully, then conflict can descend to the repositioning stage where it becomes less about finding a solution and more about protecting oneself. The question then becomes, "Who caused the problem?"

This is the beginning of the blame game. Trust begins to deteriorate as well as open communication. How would team members openly talk to each other if their interest moves from remedy to self-preservation? More likely fingers will be pointing and not much else.

If, at this stage, conflict is not resolved, it moves to **Rights**. This is where sides are created. Camps form. Factions and fractions appear throughout a group.

This is one of the fatal results of unresolved conflict: *divide*. Skirmishes become battles waged in small and large arenas.

The Honor of Fighting Fair

Instead of an atmosphere of group success and win-win solutions, the personal objective is to simply be right and prove others wrong.

The key lesson that gets lost here is that sometimes, for the sake of peace, you must simply give up the right to be right. That's a mark of genuine humility. But no one wants to do that at this stage of the fight.

Removal. When things have slipped to yet another level, it then becomes necessary to get rid of the opposition—those now seen as *adversaries* and no longer *allies*. Divorce is now the only answer in the minds of those embroiled in the ongoing, and falling conflict.

In the *removal* stage, the various camps remain, with defined leaders, and are moving from simply warring against each other to wanting to eliminate those who have become their enemies. Communication is mostly non-existent and combative if forced. No one is really talking to each other at this point.

There *are* times when toxic people need to be dismissed, but simply canceling people because you are unable, or unwilling, to respectfully resolve conflict is preventable and unhealthy.

(That's a message that needs to be broadcasted to the world.)

Sometimes you just need to give up the right to be right. That's a mark of genuine humility.

Revenge. "I don't get mad, I get even." That makes for some biting sarcasm, or a witty bumper sticker, but a terrible way of settling a dispute. It conjures images of John Rambo shooting, tearing, and otherwise blowing up the streets of a small town because he was harassed by a local sheriff. But again, that's a fictional story on a screen.

Allowing people to go *Rambo* (figuratively speaking) is a clear sign that destructive conflict has had its way. The situation has become so personal that rage sets in and people are beyond indignant. Resentment demands that someone pay. A toll must be exacted. While what form that may take will vary, the intent remains: I no longer care who's right and who's wrong, just as long as the other person suffers in some way.

The thinking is that, perhaps, it will expunge all the pent-up hostility that has now taken root. This is never the case and a horrible motive. As Emile Cioran states:

Revenge is not always sweet, once it is consummated, we feel inferior to our victim.

Forgiveness, grace, understanding, patience, and unity. These attributes are mutually exclusive to feelings of vengeance. They are to revenge as warmth is to frost on the hard ground. Heroic leaders work hard to instill these, and similar, characteristics as to not let a sliding conflict get anywhere near this stage of hostility and anger.

Heroic leaders believe conflict can and should be resolved. He or she acknowledges and proves that the work and health of the team are far too important to wallow and get absorbed in ongoing, open-ended conflict.

The Honor of Fighting Fair

But what does it mean to resolve? According to the original language the Latin word is "resolvere," which means to dissolve or disintegrate, and often with intensive effort.

Words have meaning and power. When you fully understand what it means to *resolve* an issue it can give you a deeper appreciation for what it takes to be successful in eliminating, not just nursing, a tense situation.

If there's going to be a fight, it *can* be constructive, void of personal attacks. How many issues continue to seethe and then intensify because the parties involved fought each other instead of tackling the actual problem?

Heroic leadership doesn't shy away from conflict, he or she welcomes it. But rules are set up so that regardless of the issue, it's a fair fight.

How, then does a team or individual fight fair?

- **Avoid Personal Attacks**: When people attack each other, walls get erected. When they attack the issue together, bridges form.

- **Communicate Assertively**: Honest communication is good. But being abrasive and abusive is damaging and cancerous.

- **Find Common Ground**: Remember the 85% rule. If there is 85% of something on which to agree, then drop the 15% and let the other person keep it.

- **Seek Win-Win Solutions**: While it may sound trite, it can't be discounted. The desire for the team to win must be larger than that of being proven right.

➢ **Commit to Building Relationships**: Never allow the issue to be bigger than the relationship. Seek to settle the issue, or issues, and protect the relationship.

Heroic leadership doesn't shy away from conflict, he or she welcomes it.

Conflict doesn't have to distract, or worse, collapse the daily pursuit of a group or organization. It can conversely galvanize unity and greater cooperation, if handled properly. *If* you fight fair.

Now kindly open the cage and free the gorilla.

- Conflict happens. It's unavoidable and inevitable.
- Conflict can be constructive or destructive.
- Conflict can make you bitter or better. Your choice.
- No one agrees 100% of the time. Focus on the 85%.
- Attack the issue, not the person.
- Never let the issue become bigger than the relationship.
- Resolve don't just manage, conflict. Settle the issue!

Chapter 8

THE LEVELING OF CALM

Chapter 8
The Leveling of Calm

Nothing is so bitter that a calm mind cannot find comfort in it
—Seneca the Younger.

Remember to keep the mind calm in difficult moments
—Horace.

You can't always control what goes on outside, but you can always control what goes on inside
—Wayne Dyer.

James Garfield may be one of the most underrated presidents in history. Born of simple means (he didn't even own a pair of shoes until he was four) he would eventually rise above his poor station to become America's 20th commander-in-chief.

Along the way, he would work odd jobs while reading and learning, and eventually be accepted into Williams College by the president. He would later graduate with honors and subsequently tenure as a professor at Hiram College. He then ventured into politics, serving as a congressman from Ohio, until the Civil War broke out and he was commissioned as general in the army. After performing that role, more than admirably, he returned to public service and served nine terms, again as a congressman, even becoming minority leader.

Even with all of that governmental experience, nothing could have prepared him for the unexpected that took place at the 1880 Republican National Convention. Though he was there to nominate another, he himself received that honor and went on to win a close presidential election, defeating Winfield S. Hancock, though he did almost no campaigning.

But that's not the crucial moment to which this story points to; however, being elevated to the highest office in the land would certainly classify.

With only 120 days in office, Garfield stood at a train station in Washington D.C. preparing to leave for a family vacation when a deranged and opportunistic man named Charles J. Guiteau shot him, once in the arm, and the other in the back.

While this was certainly a terrible event, filled with pain, terror, and shock, it would not be the worst that was to come. Further, many people, especially soldiers, could live to survive a bullet wound, even to the head, depending on where it lay.

Thus, the horror of being shot was somewhat mitigated by the chance that it would not prove fatal, and that Garfield would recover. A prospect that was given even chances later that night.

But what followed that fateful event is a series of agonies that one would not wish on their worst enemy, let alone a beloved president. Immediately following the attack, a team of doctors rushed to Garfield's side. While Willard Bliss emerged as the de facto lead physician, the group dynamic quickly, and continuously, became a war of opinions regarding diagnosis and treatment. The ensuing and constant bickering, and lack of unified care, brought chaos, confusion, prolonged suffering, and ultimately death.

Also, keep in mind that this was the year 1881, absent of many of the modern devices we now take for granted,

The Leveling of Calm

including the X-ray, which was introduced four years later. In addition, not only was antiseptic not used, it was derided and contradicted how doctors viewed germs and the dynamics of surgery during that era of medicine.

Attempts to find the bullet, including the summoning of Alexander Graham Bell, with an invention akin to a metal detector, proved repeatedly unsuccessful. This put more pressure on the bickering doctors to correctly assess and alleviate the wound. Imagine a team of doctors constantly poking and prodding with their fingers and unsanitary, cold instruments.

Add to that it was summer. And, while the Army Corps of Engineers would install a makeshift air conditioning apparatus, it would help only a little. Garfield literally laid motionless, sweating, and fighting infection, with a bullet still lodged in his back. This went on for 79 days, during which time he wasted from his normal weight of 210 pounds down to 130.

Seven days of this kind of agony might be too much for most of us to handle. But to a person, the comments and observations that were made about the president were that he never complained, never fussed, was never cross with any of the doctors, nurses, or visitors.

James Garfield finally died on September 19, 1881, after suffering more from infection from faulty care than the actual bullet. But through it all, somehow there was a sense of calm that emanated from him despite his suffering.

Find Calm and Lead On

Despite the danger or distress, one thing you could always seem to count on, when chaos erupted, or danger presented itself, was the hero seeming to be in control, not just of the situation, but himself. At least that's the way I remember it.

Maybe in his or her mind, or deep inside, there was an inner struggle taking place just as violent as the one on the outside, but you would never know it, as the calm assurance displayed on the outside was a source of comfort to those who were in peril.

Life happens.

No one gets to choose when moments of stress and difficulty occur. That's not news. But with that being the case, why do so many struggle with their reaction, if not overreaction, to these crucial moments? Why is it more are not able to stay composed during troubled times?

All being well, you and I will never be faced with death from an attacker's bullet. But as mentioned in Chapter 6, life can hit us as it chooses and at least dampen our spirits. We are emotional beings. When we experience the good ones such as happiness, peace, pleasure, and jubilation, life is good and so are we. But the unpleasant emotions are just as important and can't be simply ignored or whitewashed.

What does the process look like to ensure the emotions that reside in all of us don't run amok and negatively impact those around us? Certainly, there's a balance. Again, problems are common to everyone, and it would be error to pretend they don't affect you. That's not healthy.

While we can't control when bad moments will strike, one *can* control what to do with them and what happens next. This is what separates the mature leader, the heroic leader, from the average person who never rises above impulsively reacting to bad situations instead of carefully *responding*.

Make no mistake, the two choices could not be more different, as are the paths they follow. The quality of your life and the strength of your leadership will be largely determined by this choice, as will the overall tenor of your team.

Again, staying calm doesn't mean pretending that the harsh realities of life have no effect. That's denying that every day can offer a series of contrasting events. We can't eat cake all the time. While people tend to gravitate to the people, things, and situations that bring happiness, unhappy moments do occur. It's an undeniable part of living.

This makes it all the harder when an adverse event, big or small, supplants us in a way that seems abrupt and disturbs the sense of tranquility we all want to enjoy every possible moment.

> *No one gets to choose when bad moments will strike, only what happens next.*

It's in these moments that the ability to stay calm, and not let emotions control the next action or word spoken, will provide the steadfast leadership your team needs even in the most trying of times.

As Mavis Mazhura states:

Emotions can get in the way or get you on the way.

As mentioned in Chapter 2, one's attitude is a state of mind not dictated by feelings, as they are just too unpredictable and fleeting. Calm is consistent and can remain long after the crisis has passed. It is also a quieting factor that will edify the mind and soul while in the thick of it.

One can only imagine the thoughts that raced through the mind of James Garfield as he lay there day after agonizing day, but there's no record of any other tone offered by President Garfield than what was serene and gracious with his caregivers.

Only he knows exactly how he was able to find that sense of tranquility, but there are some simple, key questions every leader can ask him or herself to draw closer to a similar place of tranquility in stressful moments.

What's my current mindset?

Everyone has a filter with which we seek to interpret what happens to us. We all have a way of thinking that's shaped by our values, core beliefs, opinions, knowledge, and experience. Much goes into this *filter* and our thinking.

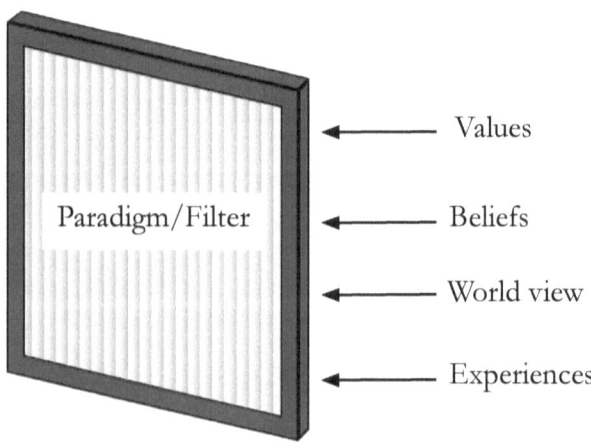

These filters can function much like those we use at home and in our cars, and like those, over time, can become clogged, dirty, and caked. This can dim our outlook and negatively affect how one processes moments of trouble or tension.

As one writer said:

Man is not affected by events, but his view of them.

A strong and sound mindset, "replaced" on a daily basis, will help one think more soundly than one that has the dirt and debris of faulty thinking.

What are you doing to keep a clear head and enrich your thoughts? The mind is so powerful. It handles billions and billions of bits of information and never gets tired. It can trap a single thought and replay it as you dwell on it, positive or negative. The thoughts we choose to rehearse can become like reruns of a bad show if not chosen carefully.

Consider what you can do to practice mind care and a healthy mindset.

> *Man is not affected by events,
> but his view of them.*

How much significance am I placing on this?

Everything has meaning, but not everything has the *same* meaning or amount of significance. Is it possible that, in some moments, the magnifying glass is used when a normal looking glass would be better? It can be easy to enlarge a problem a bit too quickly and dramatically. But to draw the proper conclusions it's important to keep things in their proper sizes. Otherwise, the "point" we want to make of what is happening will also be distorted.

Every person wants things in life to make sense. Sometimes they do, sometimes they don't. But ascribing too much import to what could be a smaller or passing issue can cause a situation to seem worse than it really is. You and I get to choose how much significance we place on certain events, good or bad. Whether it's on a number scale, letter grade, color, or other mental picture, the value of proper judging can't be understated.

> *Every person wants things in life to make sense.*

As John Sununu says:

Perspective gives us the ability to accurately contrast the large with the small, and the important with the less important. Without it we are lost in a world where all ideas, news, and information look the same. We cannot differentiate, we cannot prioritize, and we cannot make good choices.

Three clarifying questions that could help keep things in proper perspective:

1. *Is this a small matter on which I'm placing too much importance?*
2. *Is this too big a matter I'm trying to deliberately dismiss or minimize?*
3. *What does this really mean for me, my group, my organization, and those I lead?*

Extremes are always dangerous and could give emotion a free reign. Appropriately embracing reality is key. Swinging the pendulum too much in either direction fudges on "what is," the basic definition of reality.

I could walk outside on a hot day when the temperature is 101 degrees and say to myself "It's not so hot." But depending on what I do, following that statement, my body might tell me otherwise. I'll only know that after waking up from heat exhaustion.

Since reality can't be changed, the ability to face it with a solid level of emotional maturity will transform your leadership and help you be the person who remains calm while others are racing for the exits.

Judge your events carefully. You and I don't have to be bowled over by *everything*.

> *Extremes are always dangerous and could give emotion a free reign.*

Am I already under stress?

Compound emotional stress adds up, especially if disregarded. When warning signs are ignored and levels of steam continue to rise, eventually the pipe bursts. No one wants to be around when that happens.

One of my former habits, that my wife would highly criticize, was the practice of letting the gas in my vehicle deplete to almost empty before refilling. I've abandoned that with the recent fuel issues.

But we have warning lights and indicators on our dashboards for a reason. Our bodies do as well. It's dangerous, and even irresponsible, to see that life is draining our energy and not take positive action, at that time, to meet stress and not run on empty. Pressure can be your friend but not left unrestrained or uncontested.

Finding support, balance, even exercising, and the aforementioned positive frame of mind can help. Has your "dashboard" indicated any of the following warning lights?

- *Irritability*: Unless you're just generally that way. If so, go back to Chapter 2.
- *Withdrawal*: A lack of desire to be around people. Unhealthy isolation.
- *Anxiousness*: A nervous, tense sensation that won't go away.
- *Sleeplessness*: Waking up often at night and frightful dreams.
- *Lack of Focus*: Difficulty in completing tasks.

While not an exhaustive list, enough that can serve as gauges that will determine your capacity is low to handle the next stressful event.

Keep a check on your dashboard. No one runs well, or at all, on empty.

What am I saying to myself?

Everybody talks to themselves and not always with good things. Self-talk is a big deal. We all have those internal conversations (sometimes external) that impact our mood and performance.

The Leveling of Calm

Athletes practice self-talk that moves them closer to what they want to achieve. Affirmations are a key part of that and even more crucial on some of the biggest stages and competition in the world.

Andre Agassi describes it this way:

Tennis is the loneliest of sports. In golf, you play the course—plus you have a caddie—and the game ends at 18 holes. In boxing, you have a corner man and a set number of rounds.

In tennis, you're on an island, with no clock. You can't sit on a lead. You have to win the last point to win a match.

But I will say this—I can confidently say that tennis is the loneliest sport that exists. You're out there, you can't talk to anybody, you can't pass the ball, there are no time-outs. There's no coaching, you don't have to be good, you have to be better than one person and that one person is on the other side of the net.

It's like you're on an island. It's not like boxing where we're leaning on each other and you can feel each other. If you look at a tennis player it's like solitary confinement out there, and what happens in solitary confinement? It always leads to self-talk.

You have those Lincoln-Douglas debates with yourself. You talk to yourself and you answer yourself and you tell me if you've ever seen another sport where an athlete talks to themselves as much as they do in tennis.

If you're going to talk to yourself in highly pressurized situations, pick a good conversation to have and tell yourself helpful things that will lead you forward as well as your team.

> *Everybody talks to themselves, and not always good things.*

How did I start my day?

Ritual matters. How you wake up, along with those first few thoughts and actions, play a huge role in how your day flows. Instead of quiet, meditative time, too many people ravage their minds with instant news, negative thoughts, and noise.

It can be even worse if you don't consider yourself a morning person. But whenever you awaken and get out of bed, your initial thoughts and activities are a big deal.

While they vary, the greatest minds and leaders had solid morning rituals that not only set the tone for their day, but for their lives.

- ➤ **Tim Cook** (Apple) exercises after checking his email.
- ➤ **Richard Branson** also enjoys exercise in the morning.
- ➤ **Jeff Bezos** enjoys breakfast with his family before starting his days and abhors morning meetings. (Don't we all?)
- ➤ **Howard Shultz** loves making coffee for he and his wife after he walks his three dogs.
- ➤ **Anna Wintour** (*Vogue* magazine) starts her day with an hour of tennis.

At least with these individuals, it seems like exercise is an important part of waking up. But there are other important activities, as this is likely not all these individuals do in the morning.

Activities such as *meditation, prayer, reading, planning,* and *goal setting* are also solid ways to initialize each day and be well centered and truly ready to face whatever it may bring: good, bad, or otherwise.

As mentioned, no one can predict when moments of stress will occur. It would be a little easier to remain calm if we could. That's all the more reason to have strategies in place that will help soften the blow. That moment of choice makes all the difference, depending on the willingness to exercise some caution and what could best be described as personal power. Embracing reality, but with a sense of responsibility and choice. Taking just a counter moment, to not slide into the ease of simply reacting, can make a big difference when leveling your emotions in tough times.

The power is in the pause.

If and when your day is interrupted by a stressful event, find a way to interrupt the potential negative impact.

For example, take a breath, take a walk, listen to some relaxing music, shift your brain to help it rationalize and not *catastrophize*. Imagine a pleasant or humorous scene. (Yes, going to your happy place is real.) The secret is taking that moment and maximizing the power in the pause.

What bad choices and reactions could be easily avoided if that window of time were effectively employed? What needless arguments, conflict, bad acts, and the inevitable hurt feelings could have been spared if the power in the pause was exercised?

Leaders don't receive an exemption as it relates to stressful moments. The argument could be made that the higher the level the bigger the devils. This makes the ability to calmly meet these moments even more critical. Your team will follow your lead on everything, including how you will find composure in times of stress and difficulty.

The power is in the pause.

Real person: real story.

A client recently shared a story that fits here.

One day an associate was loudly arguing with his team member and threatened to return and cause harm—to "shoot up the place." Threats of violence can be jarring. But after witnessing all that one of his team members could do to rectify the situation, he simply opened the door and let the individual know he needed to leave and that he would call the police if he didn't.

With a string of mumbles, he started out the door. But didn't completely exit before turning around and spitting in my client's face.

What would you do in that moment? This heroic leader, who was in a motorcycle group, had been shot twice in his life, simply stood.

That's the power in the pause.

Seek calm and lead on.

- React or respond. Your choice.
- Remaining calm doesn't mean life doesn't hurt sometimes.
- We all have a mindset, a way we think.
- Putting too much, or too little, emphasis on a matter is not wise.
- Talk up to yourself, not down.
- Watch the warning lights. Don't run on empty.
- Start your day in a purposeful, intentional way.
- The power is in the pause.

Chapter 9

A HEART TO SERVE

Chapter 9
A Heart to Serve

Not so with you. Instead, whoever wants to become great among you must be the servant of the rest
—Jesus.

People would rather follow a leader with a heart, not just a title
—Craig Groeschel.

Heroes, among other things, are servants of the people. They are on beck and call for whenever they are needed. Whether they respond to a flashing signal in the night sky or the beeping of a special alarm, heroes drop what they are doing to help others.

In the fictional world it is the ongoing battle against villainy or to rescue innocents from some impending doom. In the physical world, the same can be said of common, ordinary people who, because of their heart to serve, put aside their time and energy to focus on others with a heart to serve, and do so in a selfless and tireless way.

Heroic leadership is not power *over* people, but power *with* people. It's paradoxical, but true greatness comes from proving to be the least, in so much as expressing a willingness to consider others as much as self.

The term servant leadership has really taken a beating as one of those concepts that sound good on paper but fails in the day-to-day grind of the workplace. Can a leader truly have a strategic and sound mind of a director *and* a servant's heart?

Perhaps there's a lack of understanding of what servant leadership is and how it's actually practiced. It's helpful not to get caught up in terminology and semantics, or simply discard an idea out of hand.

Getting in the ditch.

On a cold, rainy night a lone officer was traveling on horseback. On the way he approached a rather disturbing scene. In a trench was a soldier feverishly digging while his superior hovered over him, yelling and shouting for him to go faster. Standing *over* him. Yelling.

"Why aren't you helping your man?" the stranger asked. "I am his commander; he is my subordinate. I tell him what to do and he complies! I am not obligated to help him."

After observing this for as long as he could stomach it, the officer dismounted, removed his coat, lowered himself into the ditch and, with shovel in hand, assisted the man in finishing his task. When the job was complete, he stepped back on to level ground and walked over to the officer who had likely been watching in amazement.

Quietly and calmy he simply said, "Any time your position prevents you from helping those in your charge, in the future, please inform me and I will be happy to change your station." (paraphrased)

That traveler was George Washington.

The same person who helped win the Revolutionary War, became our first president, and patriarch of America. But there he was, digging a trench in the rain. Sweating and exerting right alongside a foot soldier to accomplish something as mundane and unglamorous as digging a ditch.

The problem with that story is, for as long as I've been telling it, I've been unable to find any verifiable proof that that truly happened. Having said that, the principle still applies: leadership is not barking orders. Heroic leadership is being willing to lower yourself to and get in the trench with your people. To serve them with a heart that cares, not just a voice that directs.

The heart of a servant doesn't belie the assertive, tough-minded leader. It doesn't make one weak or passive. The heart of a servant simply shows that a leader is, at least, equally interested in the people as he or she is in the task. Discovering and expressing ways to show you care will forge a righteous path to greatness; and not just for you, your team, but toward a lasting legacy. *Seldom, if ever, do we remember selfish leaders.*

Of course, the tough-minded leader will care about getting the job done and fulfill the mission. But do the members of the team feel and believe that they are more than just a means to an end? Or are they just another tool in the toolbox?

Do they know they have value based on how their leader treats them and cares for them?

Remember that a big component in building and sustaining trust is compassion. Who would want to work with someone who fails to understand that issues of care and human worth are non-negotiable?

Customer focus is a given. But what about employee focus and serving the team in a loving way?

As Angela Ahrendts, a senior VP at Apple states:

Everyone talks about building a relationship with your customer. I think you build one with your employees first.

Heroic leadership goes beyond simply telling people what to do and operating as some kind of positional overlord. Heroic leadership practices sensitivity to what their team needs, not just what they can do.

As a recovering "control freak" I know the consequences of focusing so much on the task you lose sight of the people. When the emphasis becomes so much about the project that people simply feel they are a number or "cog in the wheel," servant-minded culture is lost.

While it sounds simple, it's not always easy to take the time to genuinely care for the people you count on every day to get the job done.

Seldom, if ever, do we remember selfish leaders.

It's the age-old "forest for the trees" reality. How can there be time to practice the heart of a servant when there's so much to do? There is *always* time to do the right thing. And getting off your horse, demonstrating concern, and standing alongside your team in the ditch is always right. That can't be done the same way from a lofty pose.

Much has been written about the qualities and traits of a servant leader and there's no need to overcomplicate it. I think simple is best. No need for exquisite diagrams and charts, just key areas that any leader can practice showing they care and serve their needs.

Empathy—Can I relate?

It will create a distance that others will sense if they don't feel you can empathize. Sympathy is good; *empathy* is better. It's easy to say you feel sorry for what someone may be going through, and that's important. But empathy expresses that you are willing to put yourself in their shoes. It goes much deeper.

As Mohsin Hamid states:

Empathy is about finding echoes of another person in yourself.

That requires some effort coupled with awareness and understanding—being willing to walk through the crowd instead of just guiding it. Both are important and not mutually exclusive. But it is easy to lose sight of various plights of team members as so much focus is on the road ahead.

Heroic leadership can do both with compassionate support.

Listening—Not just hearing voices.

I believe God was very intentional with how many ears He gave each of us and how many mouths. Not to sound flippant, but the point should be clear; listening should be practiced more than speaking. Even the *average* leader is likely a good talker, and there's certainly a time and place for the act of conveying ideas, but listening is at least *as* important.

People want to be heard. People *need* to be heard. They want to know their voice is worth listening to.

No one has enough to say to do *all* the talking. If leaders do that, the impression can be one of an uncaring manager that's focused more on self than the people that are working hard to achieve the mission. Listening is an intentional and active choice, one that goes beyond being cognizant of the fact that there are auditory sounds floating in the air.

Leonardo da Vinci said that:

Most people listen without hearing.

I could easily say the same in reverse. Some people hear without listening. The word itself even means *take notice of and act on what someone says.* Just as it takes thoughtful and aware presence to show empathy, the same is true for attentive listening.

People feel more valued when they're listened to, *cheapened* when they are ignored. They have ideas, feedback, questions, and concerns. The thoughtful, heroic leader will stop, make good eye contact, set aside his or her agenda for a few minutes to listen. *Truly* listen.

Part of the challenge is that many listen to respond or reply, not to understand. And many times, they will not even wait until you've finished sharing your point when they do! That's called interrupting, and it's a sign of impatience, not to mention rude.

It's also an indication that listening on a deep level is not taking place.

As Hemingway said:

When people talk, listen completely.

The reason people get accused of being tone deaf is not because they can't hear, it's because they don't listen; at least not to where the speaker believes their message is getting through.

Serve your team with the gift of active listening.

> *People feel more valued when they're listened to, cheapened when they are ignored.*

Acceptance—Embracing every member of your team.

We all have similarities, and we all have differences. That's the beauty of diversity. The world *is* diverse and becoming more so every day. It is not enough to point out differences, or worse, criticize or censure people who are unlike us. Diversity can, and should, bring people together, not separate over dissimilarities.

Not everyone will fit into your mold. But they don't have to! The key is recognizing that diversity can make a group or organization stronger if the right spirit and principles are applied.

Diversity is simply *everything that makes us unique*. And unique is a good word. Just as every snowflake and every thumbprint is individually different, every person is as well.

Diversity goes beyond race, creed, and nationality. There are many dimensions of uniqueness that are often overlooked, but the truth remains: we are all different and we all have inherent value.

Society has beaten up the idea of essential value in *everyone*, but for it to apply to one, it must apply to *all*. It's too easy to stereotype and fall into prejudice, and no team can fully reach its potential if bias exists.

A saving embrace. On April 15, 1947, during a home game at Ebbets Field, Jackie Robinson, the first black baseball player in the major league, committed an error. Robinson, who is *now* remembered as one of the greatest sports figures of all time, was, at the time, reviled and hated for his act of breaking the color barrier. Thus, when the error occurred, the home crowd booed mercilessly. Typically, a player will get a pass at home with a few groans of disappointment.

It had to be both humiliating and defeating to be treated this way by those who were fans of the team, but not you as a player.

In that moment, Pee Wee Reese walked over, put his arm around Robinson, and simply looked at the crowd until it became silent.

Jackie Robinson credits that courageous act of kindness and solidarity as saving his career as he offered his acceptance.

Unity and human dignity are related. To belong, and nurture the solidarity we desire, the heroic leader will treat every team member with an attitude of what's right, not how he or she may feel. Projecting the right attitude about diversity, accepting each person, though you may not agree with every lifestyle choice, will help demonstrate a healthy view of diversity.

> *Not everyone will fit your mold. But they don't have to!*

Encourage your people.

The cynic will say that employees get affirmed every time they cash their paycheck. Of course, people get paid. But salary, by itself, is not enough to motivate individuals to higher levels. They want to know there's more, and that their work is something other than just a way to earn a living.

It stands to reason that people give more when they feel valued. Everyone is motivated in different ways, but almost everyone will choose to give a bit more effort when their efforts are not only acknowledged, but authentically *affirmed*. Stroking someone's ego is pretense. Sincerely crediting and praising is a sincere way of showing you care, that you see them and their work.

You made my day. I've spent some time in the public classroom. Years ago, while sitting in a teacher's lounge, a framed picture caught my eye. Only it wasn't a picture. It was what someone affectionately called a "Dirty Harry Award."

Heroic Leadership

If you're a Clint Eastwood fan, or even if you aren't, you might remember that in one of the aforementioned movies, he famously says, "Go ahead punk, make my day."

Now the idea is not to go around impersonating one of the toughest characters in film history. But someone had the brilliant idea of tying that phrase together to create this creative, yet thoughtful honor. While some may think it "cheesy" or gimmicky, keep in mind I saw this proudly displayed in public view.

Given that, I have borrowed this idea (as I don't think it was copyrighted) and used it in my trainings and as a manager, as a genuine way of letting someone know that not only did they "make my day," but *why*.

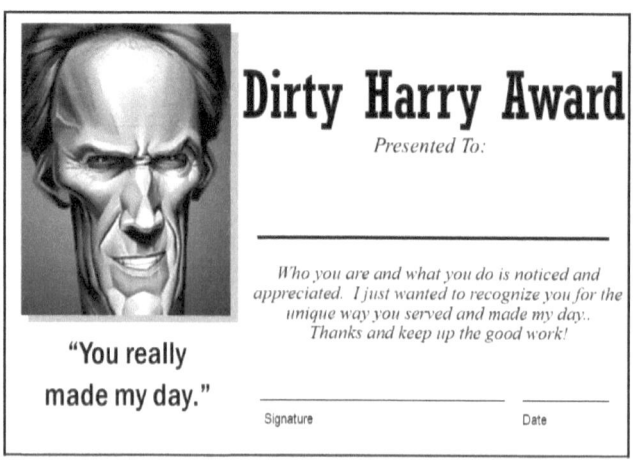

Since my first sighting of the DHA, I have seen these in offices, gracing bookshelves and desktops. Why? Because people like to be thanked and acknowledged from someone other than the payroll department. While that's certainly important, as we all have bills, we also all have a sense of pride that can be properly boosted with heartfelt affirmation and appreciation.

Heroic leaders serve their people with a full measure of gratitude.

When someone makes your day, make theirs with heartfelt thanks for what they do.

Grow them and grow with them.

One of the primary benefits to effective leadership is that of empowering those in their charge.

People want to grow. They *need* to grow. Heroic leaders will do all they can to help facilitate their journey. Growth must be championed. The ax must be sharpened on a regular basis or time will dull the edges.

What are you doing to increase the knowledge and expand the personal and professional proficiency of your team members? One hopes they would take up the mantle on their own, but remember: leadership is inspirational, not just directional.

As America's sixth president stated:

If your actions inspire others to dream more, learn more, do more and become more, you are a leader—John Quincy Adams.

The smallest spark can ignite the biggest flame. A question, a word, even a tiny bit of encouragement can provoke one to imagine he or she can become more, do more, be more.

Heroic leaders gladly fill the role of both coach and cheerleader, rooting them on, but also providing the tools and ongoing education necessary to advance.

Leaving their team members to their own devices may seem respectful, but there's a hint of laziness and apathy attached. Further, their untapped potential isn't sufficiently drawn with that kind of soft effort.

Bill Walsh, the famed coach of my once beloved San Francisco 49ers, won three Super Bowls as its head coach. But what may be even more laudable is his network tree that produced many more notable NFL coaches such as George Seifert, Mike Holmgren, Dennis Green, Sam Wyche, Ray Rhodes, and Bruce Coslet.

These, along with many more, and the players that had the opportunity to play for the originator of the "West Coast Offense," were all elevated to greater heights because Walsh was more than just a play caller. He was a teacher and a grower of people.

The time, attention, and investment you give for the growth of others will produce long-term returns for countless generations.

The smallest spark can ignite the biggest flame.

Help (when necessary).

Trench leadership may be the name of another book I write. The idea, as the story of George Washington illustrates, of rolling up your sleeves and getting your fingernails dirty to get the job done can't be overstated.

A leader can't involve at a distance, or be much of a support, when the pressure of a looming deadline is high if he or she is too far away. Weak leadership, or worse, arrogance, will say that it's below a leader to drop down and perform grunt work. "Isn't that why we hire employees?" But the secure leader, sure of who he or she is and his role, will have no problem jointly tackling whatever task, be it glamorous or not, to unassumingly help their team.

Heroic leaders won't leave them in the ditch and simply yell louder. That's not leadership. That's bossing. People want to feel leaders are by their side as much as walking ahead. It can be easier to do so in times of harvest and success. It can mean a great deal more in times of harried work and pressure.

What do leaders serve by staying on their high horse? Your soldiers are too busy to see all your fancy medals and ribbons anyway. Better to remove your coat and make it easier to grab that shovel and dig.

It all starts with heart.

People hate pretense and can usually see through a façade. Serving others, especially those you lead, has to be genuine. It can't be manufactured or mechanically practiced simply because you read it in a book (even this one).

The main question is, "Do I care about the people I've been blessed to lead, or do I only care about getting the job done?" In my own experience, I know I've fallen into the latter much too often.

The level of influence you are able to realize and enjoy will be tied to, in large part, the amount you are able to show that you do care, not just about achieving the objective, but ministering to people's spirit, their hopes, and their dreams.

That's the heart of a serving leader; the *heroic* leader. That's a heart that will touch those of others in ways that will be remembered long after the finish line has been crossed.

When people receive your sincerity and recognize your servant's heart, they will storm hell with a water pistol and climb any hill you decide to charge.

Heroic leadership is *authentic* leadership. Remember, anyone can exhaust themselves, and others, by trying to operate simply from position and a title.

Go deeper. Go further. Take people with you and serve them along the way.

Be a hero to your people. You don't need superpowers.

Lead with care and a heart to serve.

That's heroic leadership.

- No one cares how much you know unless they know you care.

- Empathy is different than sympathy. Try to walk in another's shoes.

- Listening is not hearing. Listen to understand, not just respond.

- Everyone is unique.

- People want to know and hear they have and add value.

- Growth needs a champion.

- Sometimes you have to get off your high horse and go down in the ditch.

Epilogue

The greatest leader is not necessarily the one who does the greatest things. He is the one that gets the people to do the greatest things
—Ronald Reagan.

Your story doesn't end here. It's just beginning.

With all that's been written about leadership, its meaning, examples, quotes, songs (okay, maybe not songs), what matters most is what you'll do with one of the greatest opportunities any person can have: to lead others.

As mentioned, leadership is both a privilege and a sobering responsibility. The heroic leader will balance both worlds and enjoy, not just simply *endure*, his or her role and become that hero they always knew they could be.

Potential resides in each of us. Starve your doubts and feed your confidence that you can lead others to great heights and help change the world.

No cape required.

Your journey starts now. Maybe you're new to leadership and are looking for direction. Maybe you've tried your hand at leading others and were left beaten and defeated by external forces.

It's never too late to become the leader a desperate world needs.

You can be that leader, that *heroic* leader.

I'm a big fan of asking questions. It prompts critical thinking and allows for honest soul searching.

Here are 10 questions to ask yourself as you take the lessons found in this book and apply them to your personal quest.

What's my vision? How and where do I see myself, my team, or the organization I'm leading in a year, three years, five years? While the latter may seem a bit too far, the key is challenging yourself to see ahead and take that picture of a preferable future. Are you excited about where you're headed and your image of the future? How will you get people excited about where we're headed? Have you spent time and conversation casting the vision? Remember the power of vision, how it directs, unites, motivates. Create it. Cast it. Be better tomorrow than you are today.

How committed am I to winning? Every hero knows that some battles are won, and others are lost. But no fighter goes into action thinking or expecting to lose. You can't be a winner with a defeatist mentality. The strength to win will serve as a reservoir of might that can help you prevail when the odds seem stacked against you.

Be a winner, not a whiner. Keep yourself and others encouraged. We celebrate heroes who inspired us with their confidence and poise. You can do the same for the people you lead.

Am I trustworthy? With trust being so foundational, little else will matter unless it's firmly in place. Do you have the commitment to integrity, competence, and compassion that will increase your level of trustworthiness? Do others see you as someone who can always be counted on to do what's right? Are there cracks in the armor that require attention? To follow you, people will need to trust you. They *want* to trust you. They want you to trust them.

What will you do to grow the confidence in relationships that will lead to collaborative group success? Remember, *no one climbs the mountain alone*.

Am I growing? Of course, we're all growing older, but not everyone grows up. As mentioned, not everyone is willing to pay the price and invest the time to raise the ceiling on their personal and professional leadership.

No lightning bolt is coming. To cultivate your prowess, you must be your own best advocate when it comes to the degree and sort of growth that will occur. Remember time will simply become merely tenure without rich investment in self. No one will force you. That motivation must come from within.

Don't get stuck. There's always another step to take, lesson to learn, or improvement to make.

The process is constant and should be for the rest of your life. What are you doing to maximize your growth journey?

What will be my ultimate contribution? What will be the mark and legacy I leave when I die? What will my life say? What will be the cause, or causes, that I champion and the story that I tell? *A great commitment to a great cause will build a great life*. And not just for yourself, but those you will inspire to do the same. A just cause will be a rallying cry for those who want to live for something bigger than themselves. A life worth living is a life worth living for others.

Never make a first-class commitment to a second-class cause and pursue a cause grounded in deep and righteous conviction.

Am I a carrier of hope? Can I breathe life into those I lead with a sense of hope even in the midst of the most adverse conditions and circumstance? Remember that hope is like oxygen. How long can one survive without air? How long can you survive without hope?

Part of being a hero is rousing the spirits of those who would otherwise be given to despair. Providing hope doesn't minimize or ignore the cold that life can bring. It can provide the warmth needed to somehow thrive and not just survive.

Help your crew remain focused on what is within their control and not outside of it. That will only lead to more misery. Celebrate the wins and foster a caring environment that generates communal support. Hope is not a strategy, but without it, the mission will likely be abandoned.

Do I fight fair? What am I prepared to do in order to prevent the damaging nature of destructive conflict? Do I believe that conflict can, indeed, make a team better and not bitter?

Can I lead others in having the kind of conversations that will lead to resolution, not just further divide?

Conflict is inevitable. It *will* happen. It's not always a sign of a bad relationship or situation, though it could be. Even healthy connections will experience disagreements. You can lead people to accentuate the big rocks that will keep a team cohesive and moving forward, and let the minor issues stay in the corner. Have the fight. But make it fair.

How will I handle pressure? The same boiling water that hardens the egg softens the carrot. It's not the water that's the difference, it's what's in the water.

Character is revealed when stress hits. It doesn't require much emotional or personal maturity to just react. Without pausing to consider the best response in moments of tension the path to success will not be found.

Like the center of the spinning merry-go-round at the playground, people will be attracted to a center of calm. You can provide that for yourself and for those who are struggling to keep their cool.

Remember, you are the only you this world has. Take care of yourself and you can better care for others. Which leads to the last question:

How will I serve others? Ultimately the heart of leadership is that of serving others. Without it, leadership can become static and mechanical, void of the warm human element that all relationships need, whether professional or personal.

Remember that leadership is power *with* people, not over them. Of course, you must exercise authority and provide accountability. But there's no pedestal required for that. Find ways to show that they will know that you know they have value.

Mary Kay Ash, the great cosmetic magnate once said:

Pretend that every single person you meet has a sign around his or her neck that says, 'Make me feel important.' Not only will you succeed in sales, you will succeed in life.

That's the essence of leadership.

Now go be a hero to those in your charge.

No cape required.

We can all be heroes.

SCHEDULE JIM DAVIS FOR YOUR NEXT EVENT

www.jimdavislive.com

Jim is focused, thorough, and engaging. Jim connected with his audience, used sincere and real-world examples, and gave our teams some useful perspectives and leadership tools they could use right away—Simon Nance, then Learning Manager for STIHL.

I had the opportunity to see Jim dynamically facilitate many workshops to inspire people to embrace new habits to reach greater visions. He has a subtle humor and ability to listen to understand that allows him to bring out the best in people—Marie Ringler, Corporate Trainer, Dale Carnegie.

Jim Davis

Speaking Services Offered:

2-hour Workshops   Keynotes   Half-Day Seminars

Key Topics
- High-Performance Leadership
- Building trust
- Visioneering
- Leading Healthy Conversations
- Resolving Conflict: How to Fight Fair

To contact Jim, *and receive a bonus chapter of this book*, email him directly at jim@jimdavislive.com

Notes

Notes

Notes

Notes

Notes

Notes

Notes

www.ingramcontent.com/pod-product-compliance
Lightning Source LLC
Chambersburg PA
CBHW030943180526
45163CB00002B/683